THE HOME BUYER'S INSPECTION GUIDE

Everything You Need to Know to Save $$ and Get A Better House

Warren Boroson

Ken Austin

John Wiley & Sons, Inc.

New York • Chichester • Brisbane • Toronto • Singapore

This publication is designed to provide accurate and authoritative information in regard to the subject matter covered. It is sold with the understanding that the publisher is not engaged in rendering legal, accounting, or other professional service. If legal advice or other expert assistance is required, the services of a competent professional person should be sought. From a *Declaration of Principles jointly adopted by a Committee of the American Bar Association and a Committee of Publishers.*

Library of Congress Cataloging-in-Publication Data:

Boroson, Warren.
      The homebuyer's inspection guide : everything you need to know to
save $$ and get a better house / by Warren Boroson and Ken Austin.
          p.   cm.
      Includes index.
      ISBN 0-471-57449-X (cloth). —ISBN 0-471-57450-3 (pbk.)
      1.   Dwellings—Inspection—Amateurs' manuals.   I.   Austin. C. K.
(Cyril Kenneth)
TH4817.5.B67   1993
643′012—dc20   92-31864
                                                                      CIP

Printed in the United States of America
10 9 8 7

CONTENTS

INTRODUCTION

Many people are nervous at the prospect of buying a house—with good reason.

They may be worrying: What are we getting ourselves into? Should we be descending so deeply into debt? Can we really afford it? What about all the other expenses we face—repairs, maintenance, and so forth? What if we wind up the sorry owners of a real dog—a house with a wet basement, a roof that needs replacing, a furnace about to breathe its last?

At times, it may even seem that the American dream of home-ownership is for souls braver and wiser than we are.

Fortunately, astute buyers can remove much of their fear by checking out the physical condition of a house beforehand. That's the purpose of this book: to help them evaluate the various houses they are thinking of buying—their condition, their layout, their location.

Most books on home inspection are written in technical terms, primarily by home inspectors for other home inspectors.

This book, *The Homebuyer's Inspection Guide*, is written for the average person, who may not know a septic tank from a cesspool, a boiler from a furnace, a shingle from a shake.

It was written to be read and understood by your average English teacher, tax preparer, or retail salesperson—not necessarily someone with a degree in engineering.

To help you in remembering key points, there's a series of Red Flags at the end of most chapters, warnings that a house may not be a "creampuff."

Why a book on home inspection when home inspectors are available? Because homebuyers can't afford to pay to have every house they're interested in checked out by a professional. Even though inspection fees are tiny compared with other home-purchase expenses, those fees can add up.

Solution: Armed with the knowledge provided by this book, homebuyers can give a house a once-over and ask the right questions to learn whether a particular house is worthy of further consideration. When you have compiled your list of finalists, it's time to inquire about prices and start arranging for a professional home inspection, just to confirm your own evaluation. (Besides, a home inspector won't be viewing a dream house through the rose-colored glasses that some buyers put on.)

Of course, a house's physical condition, vital as it is, shouldn't be your only consideration when you're about to buy a house. You must also consider cost, commuting distances, the quality of the school system, and so forth.

When you've narrowed your house list down to a precious few, make notes about each house's special features, its appeal, the price, taxes, and so forth. Consider taking some instant photographs of each house and its key features. (Write the address of each house on the back of each photo.) Now, number each of the finalists.

Next, rate what's important to you in housing. Give each factor below a number, from 1 (important) to 5 (not important), with 3 in the middle.

	Rating
Financial	
Asking Price (reasonableness, affordability, negotiabilty)	____
Property Taxes (Stability, affordability, rate/value relationship)	____
Energy Efficiency (Insulation, storm doors/windows, utility bills)	____
Commuting Prospects (Distance, transportation, affordability)	____
Property Condition (Systems, structure, roof, upkeep)	____
Other (_____)	____
Design	
Suitability (Style, setting, size, expandability)	____
Amenities (Yard, fencing, driveway, landscaping)	____
Bedrooms/Bathrooms (Number, size, layout, closets)	____
Kitchen (Size, appearance, lighting, appliances)	____

Attic/Basement (Size, finish,
    storage, access)   ____

Other
    (_____)   ____

General
Neighborhood (Appearance, age mix,
    community and municipal facilities)   ____

Education (Type, quality, proximity,
    transportation)   ____

Shopping (Variety, appeal, proximity,
    transportation)   ____

Recreation (Type, quality, variety,
    access)   ____

Special Conditions (Geological, flood,
    water quality, radon, climatic)   ____

Other
    (_____)   ____

Next, transfer your value ratings to the chart below. (We're assuming that you're rating five houses.)

FINANCIAL					
Price	Taxes	Energy Efficiency	Commuting	Condition	Other
1____	____	____	____	____	____
2____	____	____	____	____	____
3____	____	____	____	____	____
4____	____	____	____	____	____
5____	____	____	____	____	____

DESIGN					
Suitability	Amenities	Bedrooms/ Baths	Kitchen	Attic/ Basement	Other
1____	____	____	____	____	____
2____	____	____	____	____	____
3____	____	____	____	____	____
4____	____	____	____	____	____
5____	____	____	____	____	____

| | GENERAL | | | | |
	Education	Shopping	Recreation	Special	Other
1	_____	_____	_____	_____	_____
2	_____	_____	_____	_____	_____
3	_____	_____	_____	_____	_____
4	_____	_____	_____	_____	_____
5	_____	_____	_____	_____	_____

Finally, add up all the numbers to reach your grand totals for each house. The lower the total of the ratings, the more appealing that house probably is to you.

	Financial	Design	General	Grand Total
1	_____	_____	_____	_____
2	_____	_____	_____	_____
3	_____	_____	_____	_____
4	_____	_____	_____	_____
5	_____	_____	_____	_____

Good luck with your house hunting. We trust that reading and using the information in this book will help you choose the right house for you and your family.

I

GETTING STARTED

CHOOSING AND WORKING WITH A HOME INSPECTOR

The next home inspector you hire may turn out to be a psychic. He or she will sit in the living room of the house you're thinking of buying, feel the vibrations, and on that basis advise you whether you should purchase the place.

A psychic actually applied for membership in the American Society of Home Inspectors (ASHI) a few years ago. She was courteously turned down. But a good many people who call themselves home inspectors don't have much more in the way of credentials, reports Ron J. Passaro, who runs Res-I-Tech Inc. in Bethel, Connecticut.

Droves of people join the ranks of self-styled home inspectors every day—because they think it's a safe, comfortable, and lucrative business. But just because someone has been a plumber or likes to tinker around the house, he or she isn't necessarily qualified as a home inspector.

INCOMPETENT INSPECTORS

The fact that so many unqualified people are working as self-styled home inspectors is surely a key reason for the sudden rise in the number of lawsuits against them. "Lawsuits are increasing by leaps and bounds," reports Passaro. Here are some examples of work done by incompetent inspectors:

- One new homeowner turned on his central air conditioner shortly after he moved in—and nothing happened. The home inspector he had hired had never gotten around to trying out the system.

- Another home inspector didn't notice that the roof of a house in Glen Rock, N.J., was sagging. Also, he hadn't lifted up any panels from the dropped attic ceiling to inspect the underside of the roof. If he had, he would have seen that the previous homeowner had used guy wires to hold the roof together.

- Before Timothy and Petra Moriarty (not their real names) bought their first house a few years ago, they hired a home inspector, specifying that he inspect for termites and radon, as was required by the bank providing their mortgage. They found a home inspection service through the Yellow Pages.

  The inspection lasted 40 minutes. They paid $250 for the general inspection, $75 for the termite inspection, and $50 for the radon check. The inspector found no problems with the house, a 20-year-old colonial in northern New Jersey, except for dry rot on the siding and a leaking fitting on the boiler.

  After the Moriartys moved in, they discovered that the oven didn't work. A gas company repairman told them that the oven was probably not worth fixing.

  Almost all of the windows would not open. One window opened but would not stay up. Others opened only an inch or two. Still others flew open unless they were completely shut (the springs were too tight). Most of the storm windows needed caulking. Yet the inspector's report had stated that the windows moved freely and that the putty, caulking, and storm windows were in good condition.

  Worst of all were the termites—around the front door and in the entrance floor and closet. The Moriartys paid $938.10 to have them exterminated. They sued the home inspector for negligence and for overlooking the termites, and won a judgment of $938.10, plus fees, in small claims court. But to date they have received only $125. The company's bank account had only $26.

Of course, not all complaints against home inspectors are justified. Any homeowner unhappy with a house, for any reason, may find the inspector a convenient scapegoat.

WHAT HOME INSPECTORS DO

Only about 40 percent of homebuyers in this country use house inspectors. Perhaps the other 60 percent just don't know any better; perhaps they don't want the small extra expense ($200 and up, depending on the size of the house and the area of the country) at a time when, thanks to the down payment, they are cash-poor; perhaps they think they know enough about houses to do their own inspections; perhaps, where they live, it's just hard to find home inspectors. (See Figure 1-1.)

Inspectors can protect homebuyers against all sorts of grief as well as nasty, unexpected expenses—basements that flood, roofs that leak, termite-ridden beams, inefficient heating systems, hot-water heaters that are about to expire. What they do is check the condition of the structural, electrical, and mechanical elements of a house. While they won't tell you whether to buy a place or not, they will inform you about defects they find—and the estimated cost to repair those defects or to buy replacements.

WHAT HOME INSPECTORS DON'T DO

Many homebuyers have unrealistic notions about what home inspectors actually do and don't do. Inspectors don't estimate the

Figure 1-1.   Home inspector checking heating pipes.

market value of a house, nor do they flatly tell potential buyers whether or not to buy. They simply evaluate the various components of a house, looking for "significant defects—not stains on a carpet, a hairline crack in a window pane, or a loose doorknob," said Richard M. Weyl of St. Louis, a former president of the American Society of Home Inspectors. (See Figure 1-2.)

Many if not most inspectors don't routinely check for asbestos, termites, or radon unless they contracted to do such extra services. They don't inspect portable appliances, such as refrigerators or air conditioners. Even with built-in appliances, they don't go to the length of seeing whether, for example, an oven that's set for 450 degrees is really at 450 degrees, or that a self-cleaning oven really

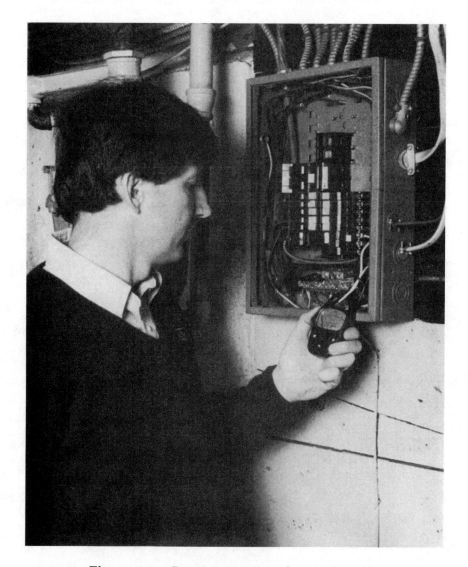

Figure 1-2.   Inspector testing electrical panel.

cleans itself. They may not check anything outside the house, such as a swimming pool or the quality and flow of water from a well. Since a standard home inspection takes about two hours to complete, there must be some limitations on items checked so there's time for the major components to be evaluated.

According to ASHI standards of practice, inspectors are not required to check the uniformity or adequacy of heat supply to the various rooms, examine the carpeting or drapes, or make sure that the roofing material complies with local codes. They also need not test every window and electrical outlet in a house—just a representative sample.

If buyers really do want the works, they can pay for an "extended-time inspection," in which the inspector is not restricted by time constraints and can check every component in much greater detail. Such extensive inspections can cost $1,500 or more, depending on the size and complexity of a particular house. Few buyers opt for so thorough an inspection.

FINDING AN INSPECTOR

The decision to have a prospective home examined may be of little assistance if you don't select the right inspection service. Just don't rely on "Uncle Louie" types; they're well-meaning relatives or friends who are self-proclaimed experts, having lived in an apartment for 30 years and done their own repairs, or having been plumbers throughout their careers. You need a real expert to determine the life expectancy of a furnace or whether a watermark in a basement means that it floods in rainy weather or just that a washing machine once overflowed. Your uncle the former plumber probably hasn't the foggiest notion whether a horizontal crack in a wall is better or worse than a vertical crack. (A horizontal crack usually indicates that there's some external force, like water pressure, at work that could cause a structural problem. A vertical crack usually is simply a sign of normal house settlement.)

Beware of unqualified inspectors. "A lot of these outfits are corporations," says Allen M. Bell, a real estate lawyer in New Jersey, "and they have no assets—just a phone, a pad, and a car they have mostly for personal use. It's cheaper to be uninsured." And if the corporation ever has a judgment lodged against it, the home inspector may open up a brand-new corporation under another name.

A few inspection companies send customers a report—after the inspection—and announce, for the first time, that their liability for mistakes is limited to the cost of the inspection or a figure like

$1,000. (Such disclaimers aren't valid because they were not made before the inspection.) More and more homebuyers are asking home inspectors whether they are insured before hiring them.

Here are other tips on finding a good home inspector:

- Reputation—Have you heard of the firm before? Has the firm been recommended by friends, your lawyer, your banker, or a relocation company?

- Experience—Find out how long the firm has been in the home inspection business. One year might be the minimum. Avoid part-time inspectors. Usually they are poorly trained and have not made the commitment to keep up-to-date on the fast-changing inspection field.

- Training—How are the firm's inspectors first trained, and what is the extent of their continual technical training? Are their inspectors certified by a nationally recognized training institute, like the National Institute of Building Inspectors (NIBI)? (See Figure 1-3.)

  Home inspectors may be engineers, architects, or former tradespeople—plumbers, electricians, carpenters, and so forth. Former tradespeople hurry to point out that an "engineer" may have studied aeronautical engineering and an "ar-

Figure 1-3.   Home inspector training center.

chitect" may have designed furniture. Most homebuyers seem more comfortable dealing with people who have extensive home inspection training and experience rather than those who have just advanced degrees.

- Insurance—A home inspection service and its inspectors should be adequately covered by liability insurance, and the No. 1 priority should be errors and omissions (E&O) insurance. This malpractice-type insurance protects the inspector (and indirectly the homebuyer and those referring the inspector) against postinspection legal problems.

  According to Gary A. Schutta, past president of the National Association of Home Inspectors, only about 5 percent of all inspectors are covered by such insurance. For companies choosing not to buy this expensive liability insurance, their only recourse in the event of a large judgment in favor of a disgruntled client is to go out of business in order to avoid responsibility for their work.

  Inspection services should also carry general liability insurance to cover personal liability not covered by the basic E&O policy. Also, all inspectors should have worker's compensation insurance. Without such coverage, the homebuyer assumes a large degree of liability for the safety and well-being of the inspector while in the employ of the homebuyer during the inspection.

- Inspection scope and duration—Find out exactly what the inspector will evaluate. Find out what the fee is for the basic inspection as well as the costs for extra services like radon testing, water testing, and so forth.

  Ask how long the inspection will take. A professional home inspection of the average house should take about two hours. Less than an hour would be worrisome.

  Be skeptical of home inspectors who don't want you to accompany them on inspections. If you tag along, they can give you valuable maintenance tips. And if you accompany them, they probably just won't zip through the house.

  On the day of the inspection, make sure the inspector is prepared to snoop into dusty attics and damp basements and even scary crawl spaces. If he or she shows up in a business suit or skirt, start worrying.

- Inspection report—Many inspection services will offer you a choice of inspection reports: a typed narrative report, or an "on-the-spot" written report for those who need information as soon as possible. Don't accept merely a verbal report. You will have no record of the inspector's actual representations, which you might want to refer to later on. (See Figure 1-4.)

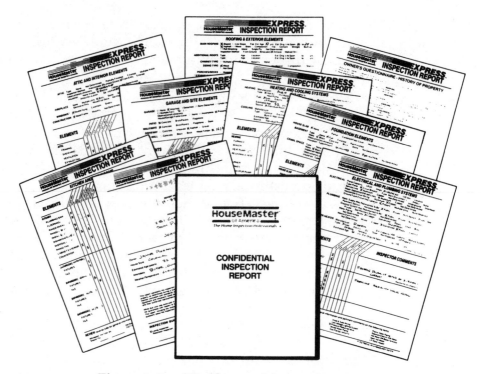

Figure 1-4.   "On-the-spot" inspection report.

- Inspection warranties—Some of the larger services offer to back up their inspectors' findings with an optional warranty, usually for one year. Such warranties add credibility to these companies' inspection reports. Inquire about the cost of these warranties or service agreements, and ask to see a copy before purchasing one.

  A warranty can be especially useful if you're selling your home and having an inspection at your own expense, just to guard against big, ugly problems that might arise before the closing. A warranty that a seller has obtained would appeal to buyers.

- Preclosing inspection—Almost all real estate contracts provide buyers with a chance to conduct one final check of the house, usually within a day or so of closing, to make sure that everything is in order and functioning. Because things can change (waterpipes burst) or undesirable conditions become apparent later on when furniture, drapes, and such are removed (holes in walls), don't overlook this step. Some inspection services will give you a special nontechnical checklist to help you perform this final house check. Other inspectors will perform the preclosing inspection for a modest fee.

WHAT THE CONTRACT SHOULD SAY

If you're signing a contract before an inspection, be sure that your lawyer inserts a clause stating that the sale is contingent upon a home inspector's report indicating that no repair or replacement above $500 is needed. The $500 figure is typical, but you can modify it upwards or downwards.

Here's a sample contingency clause, which you might review with your advisers and adapt to your own circumstances.

"This sales agreement is contingent upon receipt of a structural, mechanical, and electrical inspection of the house and a condition report by [inspection company]. The cost of this inspection will be assumed by the buyer, and the inspection will be performed within seven (7) days of the signing of this agreement.

"If the condition report reveals any structural, mechanical, or electrical defect(s) for which the cost of correcting any such defect will exceed [insert amount], the seller will have these options:

"a. effecting the necessary correction of the defect(s);
"b. negotiating the cost of correcting the defect(s) with the buyer;
"c. declaring this agreement null and void.

"In the event that the seller does not exercise any of these options, or cannot negotiate the cost of repairing the defect with the buyer, and if the buyer does not choose to ignore the defect, the buyer will have the right to declare the agreement null and void. Should either party to this agreement make such a declaration, any deposit made by the buyer shall be refunded in full. All options must be exercised within seven (7) days of the inspection date."

Some contracts provide that the seller must make repairs up to a certain amount—say, $1,000. If the seller won't go along, the buyer can proceed anyway (he or she may decide that the house is still a bargain). If neither seller nor buyer agrees to make repairs above that set amount, either can cancel the contract.

Buyers should make certain that repairs are done to their satisfaction. You don't want a roof patched when it should be replaced. Your home inspector can guide you.

IF THE SELLER PAYS

More and more sellers are paying for home inspections themselves—for good reasons:

- A last-minute house inspection, ordered by the buyer, may reveal problems that delay the closing or even cancel the sale. The home inspector may report that the roof needs replacing, that two bathrooms on the first floor have plumbing problems, or that the furnace is about to expire. The buyer may want out, even if the seller offers to make all the necessary repairs. Buyers may not be interested in a house with a basement so wet that it needs a sump pump.

  But if the sellers know beforehand about any defects, they can attend to them—or inform any buyers who come to look at the house—and not have the closing delayed or called off because the problem is discovered only later. If an inspection reveals major, costly problems, the sellers—if they don't want to take on the expense—can reduce their asking price to compensate any buyers.

- An inspection report can reassure buyers about the soundness of a house. At some point in the negotiations, you can simply say, "I had the entire house inspected a few months ago, and everything passed, except for a leaky faucet in the basement, which I had fixed. Would you like to see the inspection report? I can also show you the plumber's bill for repairing the faucet."

- In a buyer's market, when buyers have many choices, little things can mean a lot. Having written evidence that a house is shipshape, while saving the buyers a few hundred dollars on an inspection, may tilt buyers in your direction.

If buyers are interested in your house but skeptical of the inspection company that you hired, encourage them to hire their own company. Be sure that the buyers don't insert into the contract a contingency clause so vague that they can bow out on a whim (if the inspection report is "unsatisfactory," for example).

WHAT INSPECTORS CHECK

- Central heating system and components;
- Central cooling system and components;
- Interior plumbing system and components;
- Roof—structural soundness and absence of water penetration;
- Siding;
- Walls, ceilings, and floors;
- Foundation and basement; and
- Whether built-in kitchen appliances, like ovens, work.

WHAT INSPECTORS MAY NOT CHECK

- Portable appliances like refrigerators, dryers, and washers;
- Burglar and fire alarms;
- Storm windows, storm doors, and other seasonal accessories;
- Anything outside the house—wells, swimming pools, septic systems;
- Presence of wood-destroying insects;
- Presence of hazardous materials (radon, asbestos);
- Anything to do with appearance (for example, stains on a rug);
- Any area difficult to reach, like a crawl space;
- Adequacy of heat in various rooms; and
- Whether any part of a house violates local codes.

A BRIEF HISTORY OF HOME INSPECTIONS

The home inspection business began in the 1960s. In those early days, homebuilders were often asked to check out a house for a friend, or a friend of a friend, who was thinking of buying and wanted to make sure that the house was in tip-top shape.

John J. Heyn, one of the industry's pioneers and a former homebuilder in the Baltimore area, recalls some of his earliest home inspection clients: "They basically were looking for reassurances regarding the condition of their prospective homes. I would usually tour the house with them and point out anything that didn't appear to be proper."

Such simple walk-throughs gave way to specific inspection techniques and procedures. One-page summary sheets became multi-paged, detailed documents.

The formation of the industry's first society, in 1976, led to the setting of standards of practice for the fledgling industry.

Early development was slow. Real growth came in the mid- to late 1970s, when inflation drove up the price of real estate across the country. No longer was a home purchase primarily an emotional event. Economics became the motivating force. As a result, buyers wanted to know more and more about the economic commodity that was to be purchased. But the basic question was: Was it worth the price? The only way to know was to know what condition the place was in.

The era of consumerism had begun in the real estate market. Now buyers and sellers began to negotiate over any defects and deficiencies noted in inspection reports. The word spread that smart buyers—buyers who didn't want to pay too much—would always hire home inspectors.

The makeup of the industry began changing. While the early inspection market was composed mainly of one- and two-person operations, today's market has yielded to larger organizations. Smaller firms have expanded their staffs. Franchising helped give the industry increased consumer awareness and market growth. HouseMaster of America, the country's first home inspection and warranty franchise organization, was established in 1979 and remains the largest such organization in the United States.

Homebuyers of the 1990s now have a professional ally on their side to guide them in making one of the most important financial decisions of their lifetime.

Red Flags

- ✔ Your inspector is a friend or relative who once worked as a plumber or carpenter.
- ✔ The inspector claims that he or she doesn't need insurance against errors and omissions.
- ✔ The inspector doesn't come recommended by people you trust, and there's no evidence of his or her having had sufficient experience.
- ✔ He or she works only part-time.
- ✔ He or she is vague when you inquire about training.
- ✔ The inspector doesn't want you to accompany him or her.
- ✔ He or she spends less than an hour inspecting the house.
- ✔ He or she wants to give you only a verbal report, not a written report.
- ✔ The real estate agent pushes a no-name inspection service. (To placate the agent and assure that the sale goes through, the inspector might give you a misleadingly favorable report.)

2

INSPECTING THE HOUSE INSPECTION REPORT

The three chief reasons why pending house sales come unglued are (1) the buyers cannot sell their current homes, (2) the buyers cannot obtain the mortgages they want, and (3) buyers and sellers are at loggerheads over the home inspection report. In fact, many agents believe that more deals fall apart because buyers and sellers can't agree on who pays for what repair than because buyers don't qualify for mortgages.

Corey Shapiro, who owns the Maxwell Golburgh Agency in Fair Lawn, N.J., estimates that 10 percent of all sales fall through because of home inspections, whereas less than 10 percent fail because buyers can't get mortgages.

In some cases, says Shapiro, the dispute is actually the result of "buyer's remorse" or "seller's remorse." The buyers have decided that they really don't want the house (it's too small, too expensive, whatever) and use the inspection report as an excuse to bow out. Or the owners decide that they really don't want to sell and refuse to make needed repairs, just to put the kibosh on the deal.

In still other instances, a report uncovers defects so major and so expensive (the roof must be replaced, for example) that the seller goes straight into shock and negotiations over the purchase price fall apart.

Sometimes it's unavoidable that home inspections spoil a deal. But frequently the deals would have sailed through if the principals had simply understood more about the inspection reports and their purpose.

Here are some reasons why inspections kill deals, when they don't have to:

Buyers expect perfection—Fewer deals would fall through if agents explained that a home inspection is to reveal significant, hidden defects that need repair rather than obvious problems that any buyer can readily see and that have been built into the asking price—whether they be old appliances or cracked windowpanes.

Even luxurious houses tend to have flaws. Says one home inspector, "Expensive houses are bigger and use fancier materials—lots more marble in the bathrooms—but the corners are not more square or more plumb. They aren't necessarily built better.

"Even brand-new houses have flaws—things missed by a municipal building inspector who didn't test every fixture, or just plain mistakes, like no termite guards or no ventilation holes in the attic."

Yet some buyers balk at piddling problems, like loose doorknobs or thin cracks in plaster.

Buyers misunderstand—Inspection reports sometimes scare buyers out of their skins, unnecessarily.

The home inspector may recommend that the gutters be cleaned of leaves regularly. The buyer may interpret that to mean that the house has a defect when it's only a suggestion for normal preventive maintenance.

Or the inspector may recommend that groundfault circuit interruptors (which are like circuit breakers) be installed in the kitchen next to the sink or in the bathrooms. Again, this isn't a defect but something especially desirable—and the seller shouldn't be expected to pay.

Smart agents accompany buyers on the inspection tour, to reassure them. If the inspector notices a watermark on a ceiling, the agent might be able to note that the owner had mentioned that a plumbing fixture had been repaired recently.

To repeat: It's in the buyer's best interest to accompany the inspector on the inspection. Being there, the buyer will be able to discuss the extent and severity of any problems and can probably resolve much of the understandable anxiety that he or she may feel. (See Figures 2-1 and 2-2.)

Someone is stubborn—In some cases, sellers are just plain inflexible. They may feel that they're taking enormous losses compared with what they could have obtained for their houses in years gone by, so they want to sell as is, with no repairs or improvements.

One lawyer says he has seen deals fall through over $500 worth of repairs. "There are real contests, with buyers and sellers saying, 'This is it.'"

Typically a report finds one major defect and a few minor defects. Major defects—termite infestation, a high radon reading,

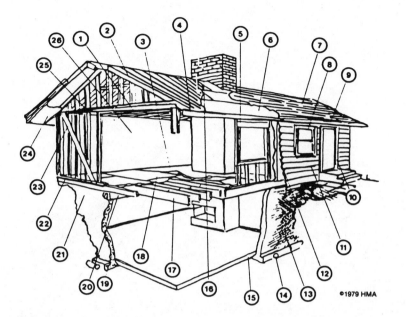

This schematic and glossary will help to familiarize you with the structural elements of your prospective home and to more readily understand the HMA Inspector and his report.

1. **Ceiling Joist** — one of a series of parallel beams used to support ceiling loads.
2. **Rafter** - one of a series of structural members designed to support roof loads.
3. **Flooring** - the interior horizontal surface of the house. May only be plywood if carpeting is used.
4. **Fascia** - a flat, horizontal member of cornice placed in a vertical position.
5. **Header** - a framing member across the top of an opening to distribute the load.
6. **Roof Sheathing** - these are flat boards that are nailed to the rafters to which is fastened the covering.
7. **Roof Covering** - the outer surface of the roof designed to withstand the elements.
8. **Window Casing** - the framing members containing and supporting the windows of the house.
9. **Gutter** - an open channel installed along the eave of a roof to take away rain water.
10. **Door Jamb** - an upright surface that lines an opening for a door.
11. **Siding** - the exposed surface of exterior walls of frame buildings.
12. **Wall Sheathing** - a sub-surface material nailed to exterior studs to back the siding.
13. **Parge Coat** - a coating of a foundation wall to retard the passage of water.

14. **Drain Tile** - an underground drainage system used to carry off excess water at foundation footings.
15. **Slab** - concrete floor placed directly on earth or gravel base and supported on the footings.
16. **Chimney Flashing** - a shield used at junction of chimney and roof to prevent leaks.
17. **Floor Joist** - one of a series of framing members which rests on outer foundation walls and interior girders.
18. **Sub-Flooring** - a wood or fibrous material that is nailed to the floor joists and that receives the finished flooring.
19. **Footing** - a concrete horizontal base on which the house foundation rests.
20. **Main Girder** - the main support that usually runs between foundation walls to carry the weight of a floor.
21. **Foundation** - construction below or partly below grade which provides support for the house.
22. **Sill Plate** - one of a series of horizontal framing members resting on top of the foundation wall.
23. **Bracing** - technique used to stiffen the building. Its use has diminished with the advent of plywood sheathing.
24. **Soffit** - the visible horizontal underside of the eave or overhang of a house.
25. **Stud** - the vertical members of the house framing to which horizontal sheets are nailed.
26. **Wall Board** - an interior wall surface of plasterboard or material other than plaster.

Figure 2-1.   Anatomy of a house.

a leaky basement—call for automatic repairs, with one exception: if the house has been advertised as a handyman's special.

Still, no one promised the buyer a rose garden—or a totally new roof or furnace (unless it's a new house). So the cost is usually shared. The sellers knock some money off the purchase price.

During negotiations over who pays for what, remember the truism, "Whoever wants the deal the most, gives the most." The

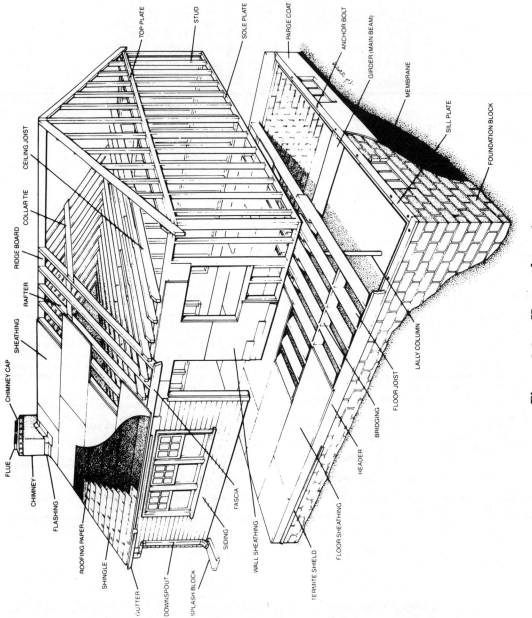

Figure 2-2. Home schematic.

18

state of the market may favor either buyer or seller. If there are a flood of houses on the market, a buyer may take a hike if the seller isn't accommodating.

Sellers may be especially flexible if they have already purchased another home and if a moving truck is coming in two weeks—and they prefer not carry two mortgages. Buyers may be especially flexible if they have already sold their houses, or if their leases are at an end and their furniture is in storage.

Negotiating tacticians suggest that a bargainer keep appealing to fairness ("Do you think it's fair that I pay for a completely new roof, even though you agree that the house is reasonably priced?") and to keep pleading poverty ("I love the house, and the price is fair, but I just can't afford to pay a few thousand for a new roof in a year or two.").

When the seller makes the repair—Buyers may be justifiably suspicious if the sellers announce that they themselves have repaired something that was amiss. The seller may have visited someone who hangs out in the local hardware store and told him, "Do whatever you can—for under $50."

Better that buyer and seller ask the home inspector what a repair or replacement may cost, run the figures by contractor or two, and then agree on what amount the seller should knock off the purchase price.

The missing ground rules—A special problem with inspection reports is that often there isn't agreement on what the ground rules should be.

Should buyers be allowed to withdraw from a contract if something is seriously wrong with a house, even if the seller is willing and able to have everything fixed? (Problems outside a house may not be correctable—for example, a house may lie in a flood plain.)

Says one lawyer, "In my view, there's nothing wrong with giving the seller the option to correct matters."

But according to one home inspector, buyers may be unenthusiastic about a French drain system to cure a leaky basement because they know that the walls would remain wet and the humidity high. They may not want to live in a house with a well that was once contaminated because the new well may need constant maintenance. And they may not want to live in a house where asbestos insulation must be removed. If removed unprofessionally, the fibers could be dispersed throughout the house.

Many contracts don't give buyers the right to withdraw from a contract if the seller agrees to make repairs. But a buyer's lawyer may insert a clause specifying that the buyer can bow out if the repairs are "major" or are above a certain amount, like $500. (See Chapter 1 for a model contingency clause.) In any case, buyers can usually extricate themselves simply by not applying for a mortgage as conscientiously as they might.

Another disagreement over the ground rules is whether the seller should be responsible for repairs if something is at the end of its "service" life.

Some observers say no. Their argument is that if something ain't broke, don't fix it. An old roof at the end of its useful life supposedly needn't be repaired or replaced so long as it's not leaking. The counterargument: Sometimes you can't wait. The roof may already be leaking into the subroofing, and the entire roof may fail at one time.

The next disagreement is whether a seller should pay for a repair that was in plain sight, such as a large crack in the asphalt driveway. The need for the repair, the seller may argue, was one reason the asking price was so low.

The buyer could argue that the house was so entrancing in other ways that he or she never noticed the crack or didn't recognize the extent of the damage until he or she read the inspector's report, or had assumed that the crack would be repaired before the house was sold.

Condos and coops—Some purchasers of condominiums or cooperatives are reluctant to pay for home inspections, perhaps to save a few hundred dollars. Sometimes their lawyers tell them not to bother. But although a condo or coop association is responsible for common exterior areas—siding, lawn, roofs—a home inspector should make sure that the common areas are being serviced and maintained properly, just to avoid future headaches.

Says one lawyer, "It's only sensible to have any large investment checked out first."

WHAT REPAIRS MAY COST

The worst news a buyer or seller can receive from a home inspector is that the foundation is failing. Repairs may cost from $6,000 to $10,000 (for rebuilding) or from $3,000 to $6,000 (for providing new support). Fortunately, foundations are in terrible shape in less than 10 percent of houses under 30 years old. (See Table 2.1)

The most *common* problem is a leaky basement, which is the case with two out of four houses. The older the house, naturally, the more frequent the problems.

Percentages of Houses with Common Problems

House Age (years)	Water in Basement (%)	Electricity (%)	Plumbing (%)
1–12	15.4	7.3	6.7
13–29	25.5	12.3	20.1
30+	32.8	18.9	25.1
Repairs and costs	Water-proofing $3,500–$5,000	Upgraded electrical service $600–$1,200	Shower pan $900–$1,600
	Sump pit and pump $600–$800	New circuits and outlets $250–$400	Water heater $350–$500

House Age (years)	Heating (%)	Cooling (%)	Insulation (%)
1–12	8.0	6.8	3.2
13–29	23.6	13.2	18.7
30+	31.0	11.3	34.1
Repairs and costs	Water boiler $2,000–$2,500	New a/c system $1,500–$2,000	Wall insulation $2,500–$3,000
	Warm-air furnace $1,500–$1,800	New compressor $800–$1,200	Attic insulation $800–$1,100

House Age (years)	Foundation (%)	Roofing (%)	Mixed Plumbing (%)
1–12	5.1	3.9	0.0
13–29	4.2	20.0	5.2
30+	8.0	27.0	44.2
Repairs and costs	Support $3,000–$6,000	New wood shingle roof $3,000–$4,00	New piping $3,000–$4,000
	Major repair $6,000–$10,000	New asphalt shingle roof $1,500–$2,200	

Source: HouseMaster of America.

Table 2.1.

3

THE CASE FOR DISCLOSURE DOCUMENTS

Some people love them. "I can't think of one objection," says an executive of Century 21. "They're good for everyone," says a real estate lawyer.

Other people loathe them. "Unnecessary paperwork," sniffs one agent. Adds a real estate lawyer, "They're just about superfluous— one additional form to add to the mountain of forms we already have."

They're talking about *disclosure forms*, documents that sellers sign revealing the awful truth about their houses—whether the basement has ever leaked, how old the dishwasher is, whether the property is in a flood plain, whether urea formaldehyde (which can cause respiratory problems) was used as insulation.

Beyond doubt, buyers can benefit from disclosure forms because they will learn what a seller knows about a house's condition.

The main problem with such disclosure forms is that most sellers don't have the technical knowledge about the true condition of their homes. Would you expect a seller to know if a foundation crack is a structural concern, if the furnace has a cracked heat exchanger, or how much longer a roof will last?

The ideal situation is to have a seller disclosure form along with an independent, unbiased home inspection report.

Disclosure forms should help dissuade sellers from outright lying. Some sellers do lie. ("All sellers are storytellers," say real estate agents.) Courts have found sellers liable for not telling buyers that their houses had recently been condemned by the board of health; that after a heavy rain a visitor would need a rowboat to reach the house; that the "pond" in the backyard was in actuality an overflowing septic field; and that a house was infested with roaches, which the buyer never saw because the place was shown only in the daytime, with all the lights blazing.

A house inspection won't cover the same ground as a disclosure form. Inspectors may not know whether improvements were made in violation of the building code, which chemicals may have been used to kill termites, and whether toxic wastes are buried in the yard. In fact, some house inspectors—including HouseMaster, the largest— have been using their own versions of owner disclosure forms since the mid-1980s and find that buyers value the extra effort to obtain additional background on their prospective homes.

Sellers presumably benefit from disclosure forms because (1) there's less likelihood that a house inspection later on will surprise a nervous buyer with an unexpected defect, and (2) the seller is less likely to be sued if a flaw—already disclosed—becomes a problem after the buyers move in. The forms may also remind sellers of what's wrong with their houses and what needs to be fixed.

Finally, it's likely that disclosure forms help to to sell houses. If a buyer is undecided between a few houses, he or she might be wise to choose the house that comes with a disclosure form. By the same token, the buyer may be more fondly disposed toward any house that the seller has had inspected at his or her own expense, or a house that comes with a warranty. (While some brokers actually report that houses with disclosure forms do sell faster, it's likely that these sellers also do other things right, like pricing their houses realistically.)

Disclosure forms are a fairly new idea. The National Association of Realtors in Washington, D.C., the trade organization for brokers, wants all state legislatures to make them obligatory. A chief reason is to protect real estate agents from lawsuits. A few courts have held the agents liable when buyers discover defects in properties that they purchased through the agents, even though these agents insisted that they weren't aware of the defects. (In one case, an agent was successfully sued simply for repeating what the homeowner had told him—that the existing well would provide enough water for the buyer's family.)

When buyers become angry, real estate agents are the obvious fall guys. The sellers may have moved to California or Florida or Timbuktu, but the agents are still available to be sued. Besides, they're sitting ducks under what the National Association of Realtors calls the "deep pocket theory" (they supposedly have lots of money).

As it is, the NAR reports that 67 percent of all lawsuits against agents in this country allege misrepresentation or the failure to disclose defects.

The solution, in the NAR's view, is a disclosure form in which the owners reveal all the dreadful defects in their houses, thus rescuing agents from the battlefield. If the owners lie, it is clearly they who are to blame, not their agents.

As of this writing, the NAR's campaign to mandate seller disclosure is beginning to pay dividends. While Maine and California have required written property condition by sellers since the late 1980s, Virginia, Wisconsin, and Kentucky have recently passed disclosure legislation. A number of other states are considering similar bills.

Coldwell Banker, one of the leading national real estate organizations, was the first company to embrace the concept of seller disclosure. The company began to require seller disclosure in all of its company-owned offices across the country early in 1992. According to Bob Swanson, Coldwell Banker's first vice president and director of administration for company-owned offices, "Our experience in California has shown that seller disclosure is right, it's good, and it benefits everyone—sellers, buyers, and brokers. The days of buyer beware are long gone."

The move toward more openness in real estate transactions signals a further strengthening of buyer protection.   Seller disclosure forms—an example of which is reproduced below—are an aid to the homebuyer. And while not a substitute for a home inspection, a prudent buyer will insist on the seller's providing one.

MODEL DOCUMENT

Property History Form

TO THE SELLER:

Please complete the following form. Do not leave any spaces blank. If the condition is not applicable to your property, mark "NA" in the blank. Attach additional pages if additional space is required.

As of _____, the following is a property history statement, made by the seller, of information concerning the condition of the property located at _____. This information is not a substitute for any inspections or warranties the purchaser may wish to obtain.

THE FOLLOWING ARE REPRESENTATIONS MADE BY THE SELLER AND ARE NOT THE REPRESENTATIONS OF SELLER'S AGENTS:

APPLIANCES/SYSTEMS:

Are the items below in working order?

	Yes	No	Age (if Known)
Range/oven			
Hood/fan			
Refrigerator			
Washer/dryer			
Central air			
Attic fan			
Ceiling fan			
Fireplace, chimney			
Garage door opener and remote controls			
Water softener			
Microwave			
Dishwasher			
Disposal			
Trash compactor			
Hot-water heater			
Sump pump			
Pool			
Central vacuum			
Security system			
Intercom			
Other			

Explanations of "No" responses; remarks, if any:

_____

_____

PROPERTY CONDITIONS AND IMPROVEMENTS:

1. Basement: Has there been evidence of or problems with water leakage? Yes ___ No ___
If yes, please explain, describing the frequency and extent of the problem:

_____

2. Has urea formaldehyde insulation (UFFI) been installed?
Yes ___ No ___ Unknown ___

3. Asbestos: Is asbestos present in any form on the property?
Yes ___ No ___ Unknown ___ If yes, where? _____

4. Roof: Age of roof ___ Leaks? Yes ___ No ___ Unknown ___ If yes, please explain, describing the frequency and extent of the problem.

_____

History of repairs: _____
5. Septic tanks/drain fields or city sewer system? (Circle) Any known service or repairs? _____

6. Heating system: Type _____ Age of system _____ Any known problems or repairs? _____

7. Plumbing system: Any known problems or repairs? _____

8. Electricity system: Capacity _____ Any known problems or repairs?_____

9. Are you aware of a fuel oil storage tank on the property? Yes ___ No ___

10. Is the property in a flood hazard area? Yes ___No ___

11. Is the property in a wetlands area? Yes ___ No ___ Unknown ___

12. Have room additions, structural modifications, or other alterations been made without necessary permits or licensed contracts? Yes ___ No ___ Unknown ___ If yes, describe: _____

13. Is the water supply from a well or municipal? (Circle)

OTHER ITEMS:

14. Is there a homeowner's association or group that has any authority over your property? Yes ___ No ___ If yes, describe:

_____

15. Are you aware of any past, present, or proposed structure or use that might create an environmental problem in your area—like a dump or landfill? _____

(You might add your own questions—about termite or insect activity, easements or restrictions, about tragic events that have occurred in the house, and so forth.)

4

THE INS AND OUTS
OF WARRANTIES

If you're buying or selling a home, you have two types of warranties (or service agreements) available.

Several home inspection companies offer postinspection plans that cover a house's mechanical systems as well as the roof and structure, depending on the condition of the house as noted in the home inspection report. For example, if an inspector considers a roof to be in a less-than-satisfactory condition, the roof would be excluded from coverage. The cost of these inspection warranties is usually $200 to $300.

The more widely available warranty is the non-inspection type. It covers only the mechanical systems of the house, and requires no professional inspection of the covered components. A real estate agent completes a plan application, which indicates that the components are in place and operating. Like disclosure documents, non-inspection warranties aren't a substitute for house inspections. They don't protect you against a basement that floods, a roof that leaks, or woodwork that has been gnawed away by termites. They're not even a substitute for home insurance. If your house burns down or burglars make off with your silverware and jewelry, a warranty won't help.

But that doesn't diminish their appeal.

Not long ago, a buyer was about to purchase a high-rise, customized condominium in the New York City area. Suddenly he began worrying. The whirlpool didn't always work. The dishwasher had a huge dent in the door. For this he was paying $600,000? Then the broker spoke the magic words: The seller would provide the buyer with a warranty, to cover the cost of repairing or replacing the mechanical systems for a year. It was a done deal.

Understandably, buyers like warranties. ERA, a national broker-age chain based in Overland Park, Kansas, has found that ERA houses with warranties sell 22 to 23 days sooner than houses without them, and for prices that are 1.5 percent higher.

Certainly more and more homeowners are jumping on the band-wagon. Nationwide there were 282,226 warranties in effect in 1986, reports the National Home Warranty Association, a trade group. In 1991 there were 516,358—an increase of 83 percent.

Throughout the country, from 8 percent to 10 percent of all homes for sale carry warranties, estimates Larry A. Reiners, executive vice president of Homeowners Marketing Services in Hollywood, Flor-ida, the second largest warranty company. In five years, he predicts, 40 percent to 50 percent of all houses for sale will have warranties.

Warranties protect buyers and sellers against mechanical fail-ures—washing machines that don't wash, driers that don't dry, sump pumps that don't pump. Portable appliances such as window air conditioners aren't covered. (Otherwise, a sneaky homeowner might bring in his mother's dying air conditioner and stick it in a window.)

Typically the broker must check that all systems are go before the warranty company will insure them. ERA is unusual in that it will protect systems with problems that obviously preexisted, so long as there's no evidence that the homeowner knew about them.

THE PROS OF WARRANTIES

For buyers, a warranty's chief benefit is that it may keep them from having to spend money when they're short. "The average first-time homebuyer doesn't have two nickels to rub together," says Jerome Strauss, president of ERA's home warranty division. "He's paid for points, a survey, title insurance, legal fees, and now he's completely stretched. His greatest fear is that the house will have an expensive mechanical failure. A warranty will give him peace of mind."

Usually the seller pays for a non-inspection warranty, though buyers can do it on their own. The price ranges from $300 to $500, with a $50 to $100 deductible per claim. Coverage lasts a year from the closing. The buyer can then renew it.

Another benefit for buyers is that repairpeople are more likely to be reliable. The warranty companies usually obtain names from brokers, and repairpeople who want steady, repeat business must mind their p's and q's. Some warranty firms regularly survey brokers or homeowners and promptly dump any repairpeople whose cus-tomers are dissatisfied.

If a system isn't worth repairing, the homeowner can apply the estimated cost of a repair to the purchase price of a replacement. For example, you can take a $1,100 estimated repair bill and apply it to the cost of a new furnace.

Most warranty companies provide a 24-hour-a-day, seven-day-a-week hot line, and will send a repairperson immediately in an emergency (if the heating breaks down in winter, for example).

Sellers aren't left out in the cold. They get almost the same coverage—typically the heating and cooling systems are excluded—from the time they list a house to the closing. Usually they need not pay until and unless the house is sold.

Of course, sellers may also benefit if it's true that houses with warranties sell faster and for higher prices. Beyond that, a warranty can be a good bargaining tool, especially for the owner of an older house. If the buyer insists that the seller shave a few thousand dollars off the asking price because the appliances are old, the seller can offer to provide a warranty instead.

Brokers and agents benefit because some sellers will list with them if they offer a warranty, and the offer of a one-year warranty on a listed house can improve the house's appeal.

WHO OFFERS WARRANTIES

The five largest warranty firms belong to the National Home Warranty Association. They are the Homeowners Marketing Services, ERA, American Home Shield in Carroll, Iowa, Guaranteed Home Inc. in Lake St. Louis, Missouri, and United One Home Protection Plan in Columbia, South Carolina. Another franchiser, besides ERA, that provides its own warranty plan is Realty World, based in Fairfax, Virginia.

The plans can differ significantly. Some have limits on the total payments they will make for any one system, such as $1,500; ERA has no limits. Homeowners Marketing Services won't write policies for homeowners selling their houses directly; American Home Shield will.

The plans also differ somewhat on which systems are covered and which aren't, and may differ on coverages for buyers and for sellers.

CHOOSING A WARRANTY

A buyer shouldn't let a warranty tip him or her toward one house or another. If you're undecided between two houses, choose the house you prefer and ask the seller to lower the price by $300 to $400, so you can pay for a warranty. (If the house has passed a professional inspection, all the systems should be working and a warranty plan should cover them.)

Decide what items you definitely want coverage for—an old refrigerator, an old hot water heater—and make sure that the warranty doesn't exclude them.

More advice for buyers:

- Make sure you can get emergency service coverage.

- Check that your heating and cooling systems are covered. They're the most expensive to repair and the most likely to break down.

- Check into limits. The best time to learn about a $500 limit on a heating system replacement is before you buy the policy, not when your $3,000 heating system breaks down.

- Find out what isn't covered. Some contracts are riddled with exclusions, says one broker. "The contract may say, 'All the plumbing is covered except for valves, faucets, union joints, and fixtures.' Well, what's left?"

Of course, sellers should choose a broker because of their confidence in that broker or agent's skill, knowledge, experience, honesty, and conscientiousness. But if they're undecided among such paragons, they might give a point or two to the one who offers a good warranty plan—especially if the seller's house is old (30 years and beyond) and the mechanical systems are also old.

WHAT A HOME WARRANTY MAY COVER

A typical non-inspection home warranty insures only the mechanical systems of a house, not the structure (not a leaking roof, for example). It covers major mechanical systems (like the heating system) only for buyers, not for sellers. Generally, portable appliances are not covered.

The dollar amounts shown below are average repair costs paid in 1989 under a Homeowners Marketing Services warranty. For each claim, the warranty holder pays $100, no matter what the cost of repair. An HMS policy that covers the items listed, for a one-family house, costs in the $350 range.

Covered for Seller and Buyer

Built-in microwave oven	$263.49
Built-in trash compactor	308.45
Central vacuum	407.26
Ceiling fans	290.34

Clothes dryer or washer	$252.05
Dishwasher	253.14
Electrical system	347.57
Garbage disposal	245.55
Garage door opener	242.77
Hot-water heater	374.00
Oven	290.57
Range	294.59
Plumbing system	333.55
Refrigerator	299.63
Water softener	490.43

Covered for Just Buyer

Central air-conditioning	433.86
Heating system	533.66
Built-in air conditioners	433.86

II

ENERGY EFFICIENCY

5

THE ENERGY-EFFICIENT HOUSE

Should a house be light colored, to reflect the summer sunlight, or dark colored, to absorb the winter rays?

Should your house be tightly insulated, to keep it cool in summer and warm in winter, or might that trap radon?

Should you use your attic fan during the summer to cool the house, or is that a waste if the attic is ventilated and the floor insulated?

The answers, as it happens, are in dispute. But the consensus seems to be: light-colored houses, tightly sealed houses, and attic fans.

THE CASE AGAINST AIR CONDITIONERS

Where the experts unanimously agree is that air conditioners are the bane of energy efficiency. The machines are great for removing moisture from the air—and money from your pocket. In fact, to a large extent home energy conservation means using air conditioners as sparingly as possible. If you're considering a house for sale, bear in mind that the more air conditioners you see in the rooms, the higher your monthly electrical bills will be.

Although air-conditioning is one of the twentieth century's blessings on humankind, it's your most expensive use of electricity. Three room air conditioners, with low EERs (energy efficiency ratios) of 6.5 and used 400 hours per cooling season, might cost as much as $375 during the summer in a state like New Jersey. A central air-conditioning system with a low SEER (seasonal energy efficiency ratio) of 7.5 might cost $361 for the season.

So the goal of any budget-minded, environmentally aware homebuyer should be to seek out houses that aren't especially dependent on air conditioners for keeping their inhabitants cool.

Tree, Vines, and Shrubs

For shading the house in summer, think of deciduous trees—trees that shed their leaves every year—on the southern and southwestern sides of a house, or near any windows exposed to a lot of sun. (Trees that lose their leaves in the fall will let the sun in during the winter.) The trees of choice are maples, oaks, ash, or other trees with full foliage on top, and not willow, box elder, or poplar, which are easily damaged by storms.

For the northwestern and western sides, think of evergreens, to protect your house from wintry blasts. Be sure to check where winter winds actually flow around your particular house.

A row of trees should extend 50 feet beyond the ends of a house. Hemlocks or firs will do; avoid pines, because their branches are high off the ground. Plant trees two or four feet tall in the autumn, and they will provide an effective windbreak in short order. (See Figure 5-1.)

Don't have a forest of evergreens surrounding your house. Houses like that may become damp and mildewed because the sun gets little chance to dry them out.

Figure 5-1.   Trees as an effective wind barrier.

If your home needs shade right now, think about planting vines on the southern or southwestern walls. Good choices would be wisteria, bittersweet, and Boston ivy, which lose their leaves. Avoid English ivy and other evergreens—unless you plant them on the northern or northwestern sides of a house, just for winter protection. And because vines may harm the siding of a house by pulling away the boards, consider growing them on trellises or latticework. (See Figure 5-2.)

Dense shrubbery next to your house would be helpful. It insulates by creating dead air space.

Overhangs, Awnings, and Shades

Ideally, a roof will have an overhang, to block the sunlight from walls and windows. The overhang won't obstruct much sunlight in winter; winter sun, unlike summer sun, is not so directly overhead.

Figure 5-2.   Damage to siding caused by vines.

Awnings should be aluminum and not canvas. Aluminum awnings will reflect heat away; usually they have openings, too, to let heat escape underneath. They should be installed on the eastern and western sides of a house, which get the most sun.

Tinted windows are also a good idea—to keep sunlight out in summer and to reflect inside heat in winter.

Colors

Why light colors all year long? Because there's a great difference between the desirable temperature inside and outside the house during the summer and during the winter. If 70 degrees inside is desirable, your attic might be 150 degrees in summer—a difference of 80 degrees. In winter, the temperature is typically 30 degrees outside in the North—a difference of only 40 degrees.

Insulation

Insulation is used mainly to reduce the rate of heat transfer from areas of high temperature to those of lower temperature—from inside the house to the outside (in winter) and from outside the house to the inside (in summer).

The ability of a material to slow this movement of heat is its "thermal resistance," or R-value. Insulation materials are rated on the basis of this R-value. The higher the R-value, the longer it takes for heat to move through the material. Insulation affects all three kinds of heat transfer: conduction, convection, and radiation.

Besides increasing heat loss or gain in a house, insulation also helps the people inside feel comfortable, lowers noise levels, reduces the size of heating or cooling equipment a house needs, and helps minimize energy costs.

But to be effective, the insulation must be the proper type. It must have adequate thermal resistance for the location. Also, it must be properly installed.

Most building codes specify the minimum insulation required (or the maximum heat loss or gain allowed through a particular building component). The way insulation is placed should be in accordance with building code guidelines and manufacturer recommendations.

Since the mid-1970s, the insulation of new homes has been standard. And the retrofitting of older homes with insulation has become financially worthwhile because of increasing fuel costs. Houses built before 1970 generally had minimal amounts of insulation; before 1940, any insulation was rare.

In general, insulation should be applied in all spaces or openings between heated or cooled areas and unheated or uncooled spaces ("conditioned"=heated or cooled). (See Figure 5-3.)

Figure 5-3.   Insulation in floor of unfinished attic.

These spaces include:

- The ceiling above conditioned spaces;
- Walls next to unconditioned spaces;
- Heated basement walls (to below grade);
- Floors above unheated crawl spaces, basements, and garages;
- The edges of slabs;
- Ductwork and pipes in unconditioned areas.

Don't overlook the access door to attics or unconditioned areas that should be insulated to keep hot or cold air from escaping there. The visible insulation should be checked for damage from moisture, compression, and so forth.

The amount of insulation needed in a house varies with the location in the house and the area of the country. Each type of insulation has a different R-value per inch of thickness. In general, the more extreme the temperatures, the higher the recommended R-value.

R-19 is the minimum ceiling insulation for all areas of the country; R-11 is the minimum for outside walls. To learn the exact R-value recommended for your area of the country, speak with someone at your local building department.

The greatest benefit from insulation usually comes with the first two or three inches. Greater amounts certainly help, but the payback in fuel savings starts declining. Incidentally, squeezing six inches of insulation into a three-inch space doesn't provide the resistance you might expect. Because of the compaction, there is greater heat loss through conduction than if three inches of insulation had been placed in a three-inch space.

You cannot readily determine the types of characteristics of insulation within a house because you cannot always get access to the insulation. Sometimes the type of insulation is mixed, too. Sometimes it's even hard to determine the actual composition of any insulation without a laboratory analysis.

Here are the major types of insulation:

Rock wool—Manufactured from extruded rock or slag fibers. Odorless and inorganic (never living, unlike wood, for instance); resistant to decay, fire, and insect damage. Used in blanket or loose form. Probably the most common type of insulation prior to 1950. R-2.2 to 3.1 per inch.

Fiberglass—An inorganic material made from fibers extruded from glass. Resists decay, fire, and insects. Most commonly used insulation since the 1950s. More resilient than rock wool, so worries about compaction are less. R-2.2 to 3.1 per inch.

Mineral wool—Generic term for fiberglass and rock wool.

Cellulose—A loose insulation generally made from scrap paper or wood products. Organic and combustible—and subject to decay, insect attacks, and water absorption. By law, must be chemically treated to improve its fire resistance. Older installations, especially before 1979, may not have been treated properly. Cellulose will settle or become compact, and thus lose its effectiveness. R-3.1 to 3.7 per inch.

Perlite—A loose insulation used mainly to fill voids, especially with masonry wall construction. Inorganic, noncombustible, and moisture and decay resistant. Made from aluminum silicate, which is crushed and heated, so small air pockets form. R-2.5 to 2.8 per inch.

Vermiculite—A mica-like material found naturally. Expands rapidly when heated. Used as a loose fill. Organic but noncombustible, and resists decay and insect attacks. R-2.0 to 2.2 per inch.

Polystyrene foam—Available in loose pellets, molded beadboard (Styrofoam), or as an extruded board. It's an inorganic polymer, but combustible. Resists decay, moisture, and insects. Most commonly used as wall sheathing or foam insulation. R-4.0 to 5.0 per inch.

Polyurethane and polyisocyanaurate foams—Available as rigid boards, formed in place, or sprayed-on applications. Flammable and subject to size changes with curing and aging. R-3.6 to 6.0 per inch.

Urea formaldehyde foam—Inorganic foam pumped into wall openings, most commonly in old, uninsulated houses. A foaming agent and hardener are usually mixed on site, and the insulation expands as it cures within the wall opening. A serious concern with this insulation has been the "outgassing" of formaldehyde, which can cause illness. But after five years, the level of outgassing usually sinks substantially. R-4.0 to 4.1 per inch.

Other insulation materials include corkboard, fiberboard, reflective barriers, wood fibers, asbestos, and even old newspapers.

Inspect the vapor barrier (a watertight material that keeps moisture in one area and out of another). Usually vapor barriers are made of foil, plastic film, or treated paper.

Most insulation relies on trapping air inside thousands of tiny pockets. These pockets limit the passage of heat. If there weren't a moisture barrier, hot air would soon permeate the insulation, condense into moisture, and reduce the insulation's effectiveness—and possibly cause structural damage.

In cold climates, vapor barriers should be on the warm side of an insulated area, toward the living area. In an unheated attic, the barrier should be on the bottom.

You need only one vapor barrier. A second layer above or adjacent to another may trap moisture.

Here are a few additional points of interest with regard to insulation:

- Some types of insulation contain materials that may be a health or enviromental concern. Individuals respond differently to these materials, and hypersensitive people will be most at risk. See Chapter 6.

- Chimneys and heat-producing recessed light fixtures should not be surrounded by insulation. You want the heat to escape, not build up to dangerous levels. Generally, a two- to six-inch clearance is required, unless the insulation labeling states otherwise.

- Insulated areas need adequate ventilation, to prevent the buildup of excessive heat or moisture. Be especially careful of cathedral ceilings, finished attics, and attics with blocked or insufficient air circulation.

- All hot-water pipes and heating ducts in unheated parts of a house should have insulation, preferably one or two inches.

- Insulation is sometimes blown into walls without there being a barrier for house moisture, causing the insulation to rot and damage the electrical wiring.

- Feel your hot-water heater. Is it warm? Insulate it with a cover you can buy in a hardware store. But leave the tank top and the controls uncovered.

Energy experts don't recommend insulating the walls of existing houses, except possibly for two-story homes. It may not be worth the cost, and it may not do the job.

Where insulation is needed especially is in the attic floor, to prevent heat from escaping in the winter or entering in the summer. But that insulation is better at doing the first than the second, which is why an attic fan may help. (See Figure 5-4.)

A ventilated attic may help reduce the temperature in summer, but—more important—let moisture escape in winter. Otherwise, moisture can damage both the insulation and the wood. Automatic power ventilators should be used, particularly where there's little natural ventilation.

Trying to find which areas of a house are insulated, and with what and how much, can be difficult. But sometimes you can spot the insulation in an attic, near the electrical outlets in a room, or on basement ceilings.

Figure 5-4.   Attic vent fan.

The insulation—whether loose fill, batts and blankets, or rigid board—should not have anything heavy on top, or it may lose its effectiveness. It should be tightly fitted into the areas it's in. (See Figure 5-5.)

A rough check for insulation is to feel an outside wall on a cold day when the furnace is on. If the wall is much cooler than the air in the room, you need more insulation.

Fans

Engineers have doubts about whole-house fans, which draw air out of the home. The devices are ideal when the air cools down at night, so you can replace the hot air inside of the house. Trouble is, if it's hot outside during the day or night, a whole-house fan will just suck

Figure 5-5.   Evaluating insulation in unfinished attic.

in hot air. In general, whole-house fans haven't made all their owners happy campers.

Room fans, either set in windows or movable, have the same failing: If it's hot outside, they will just draw in hot air. Still, they can create air movement that will evaporate perspiration and make people feel cooler.

Ceiling fans can also help people feel cooler, by circulating air. Unfortunately, they can also make people feel cooler during the winter. On cold days they work best on cathedral ceilings, where warm air may get trapped.

You can adjust many room conditioners so that they act as fans. But they mainly circulate air: They are not so effective in exchanging air.

Air Conditioners

Room air conditioners are more efficient than central, simply because you can use them only in areas you want cooled. Three large air conditioners may cost the same as central air-conditioning (providing that you already have ductwork for forced-air heating).

But replacing one room air conditioner will cost only $300 to $500, whereas the compressor on central air will run $1,600 to $1,800. Also, if your central air goes on the fritz, your entire house may become uninhabitable.

The advantages of central air are that it's quiet, it keeps an entire house cool, it doesn't blast air directly at you, and you can still open and close all your windows.

If you're trying to decide between two houses, one of which has room air and the other central air, your choice may depend on how many hours you are at home during the day. If you're at home most of the day, occupying primarily one room, a room air conditioner may be far more economical.

In using room air conditioners, keep them on a single setting. Try to avoid the maximum settings. If you want a temperature of 72 degrees, don't set it on 68—it will take just as long for the temperature to drop to 72, and you'll waste money as the temperature drops to 68. You'll end up playing temperature yo-yo. Start cooling an area early, so you don't feel forced to use the highest setting.

As a rule you need 25 to 30 British thermal units (BTUs) for each foot of space you want to air condition.

Look for air conditioners with high EERs. They should pay for themselves quickly. An air conditioner with a high rating of 9.5 may cost $86 a summer vs. $125 for one with a rating of only 7.5.

General Advice

The British journal *New Scientist* reports that water is 265 times more cooling than cold air. So your best solution for beating the heat may just be a cold bath, a swim, or wearing a wet T-shirt in front of a fan.

WHAT YOU'LL FIND IN AN ENERGY-EFFICIENT HOUSE

Here are energy-savings featurs to look for in a house:

- Vents or windows in the attic, to allow for an exchange of air in summer and the release of moisture in winter.
- Insulation in the attic, to retain warmth (and coolness) in the rooms below.
- Insulation and air infiltration barriers in walls.
- Roof overhangs and awnings, to shade a house.
- Trees and shrubs, to absorb heat and evaporate water; also to create air movement in summer.
- Light colors, to reflect heat.
- Windows that are well-sealed, with caulking and glazing; ideally, they are storm windows or with double-paned glass.
- Window fans or movable fans.
- Storm doors to keep out cold in winter.
- Ceiling fans to circulate air in the summer.
- Room air conditioners with high energy-efficiency ratios (9 or more).
- Insulated ducts in non-living areas, to retain warmth or coolness.
- Trees to shade the house in summer and protect it from wind in winter.

Red Flags

- ✔ A house full of room air conditioners may have high electrical bills, especially if there are no trees, shrubs, vines, tinted windows, awnings, or insulation to protect it from sun.
- ✔ Be wary if any house in a northern area doesn't have adequate insulation in the ceiling above conditioned spaces; in walls next to unconditioned spaces; in heated basement walls (to below grade); in floors above unheated crawl spaces, basements, and garages; in the edges of slabs; and in ductwork and pipes in unconditioned areas.
- ✔ Worry if a vapor barrier has been installed incorrectly—toward the inside of the house. It may have caused damage.

✔ An attic that isn't ventilated may be too hot in summer and be so moist in winter that the wood gets damaged.

✔ Be wary of insulation that is tightly packed down. It may have lost much of its effectiveness.

⊘ If you touch an outside wall on a cold day, with the heat on, and it's much colder than the air in the room, the insulation may be inadequate.

✔ If a house has no storm windows and doesn't have double-paned glass, check the heating bill carefully.

✔ All-electric houses require more insulation. Without the proper insulation, utility bills will be astronomical.

III

HEALTH HAZARDS

6

ASBESTOS, RADON, LEAD, SAFE DRINKING WATER

ASBESTOS

As if radon, urea-formaldehyde insulation, lead-based paint, germ-laden humidifiers, and electromagnetism from outside wires and electric blankets weren't enough to scare you out of house and home, there's always asbestos. In fact, alarm over asbestos has reached such intensity that now there's even a name for it: fiber phobia.

Some homeowners with asbestos products in their basements are so terrified that they won't even go down there anymore. Some homebuyers refuse to consider any house that has asbestos materials in it—anywhere.

Now, unquestionably, breathing in asbestos can and has caused lung cancer and respiratory disease among asbestos workers. Asbestos can also present a terrible problem for certain homeowners. A couple in Jasper, Florida, Marvin and Carol Selph, were having their home renovated a few years ago when the workers cut into asbestos wallboard, releasing fibers all over the house. The Selphs abandoned the place.

Ridding the house of asbestos, they learned, would cost $24,000. They put the house up for sale and, although the place would normally have been worth about $33,000 (the house is tiny), they received just one offer, for $5,000. Fortunately, the Selphs received a settlement from their insurance company for one-third the house's value.

Still, most asbestos experts insist that, in small amounts, asbestos fibers are not a serious health hazard. If you walk along any street, especially near a busy intersection, you'll probably inhale more asbestos from the brake linings of cars than inside your home.

The consensus of the experts is that if it ain't broke, don't fix it. If the asbestos in your house or a house you're thinking of buying is locked in place—it's "nonfriable" (not crumbling)—it poses little or no danger. In any case, the cure may be worse than the disease. The process of removing the asbestos may disperse the fibers into the air, where they may remain for weeks or even longer.

Asbestos can be found throughout many older homes, from the basement to the attic. The most likely places to find problems is on heating boilers and insulation. (See Figure 6-1.) Hot water or steam pipes may be surrounded by a blanket of asbestos and cardboard; the blanket itself can easily be damaged. The mushroom-colored insulation around the furnace may also contain asbestos. Less subject to damage is the thin, asbestos-insulated paper that may be taped on air ducts.

Although asphalt floor tiles may also contain asbestos, it's usually locked in place. You should become concerned only if it's chipping. Some acoustical material sprayed on ceilings may contain asbestos. White, crumbly insulation in the attic also may be asbestos.

Determining whether material actually contains asbestos is difficult. Unless you can find a label or call the manufacturer, you'll need

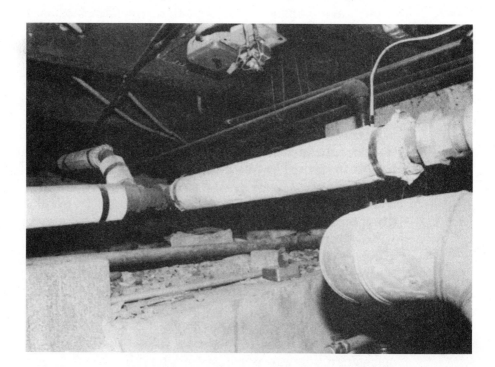

Figure 6-1.   Asbestos-covered pipes.

a laboratory test—ideally of samples from two areas of the material. Says one engineer, "Sometimes even I look at some insulation and say, 'It definitely contains asbestos.' Then a lab says no."

Since the early 1970s, less and less asbestos has been used in construction.

Although the general rule is that you should let sleeping asbestos lie, there are times to take precautions:

- If the material that may contain asbestos might be damaged— Dampen the area with a spray to keep any fibers from floating into the air, and call in professional help.

- If repairs or renovations are being made—Many remodelers and repairpeople don't take proper precautions, and may saw into or grind down vinyl-asbestos tiles or knock against asbestos-covered pipes. Make sure the renovators are educated about the danger of asbestos. They should know enough, for example, to lay new asbestos-free tile over old tile that may contain asbestos, rather than ripping up what's already in place.

- If you're buying household materials—Although the use of asbestos is being phased out, older products may still be on the shelves.

- If you're selling a house—Some buyers automatically reject a house if it seems to contain asbestos—especially young, first-time homebuyers. Older buyers may not mind.

If you're having an inspection performed—either because you're a homeowner or a homebuyer—keep in mind that it's usually better to have one asbestos expert do the inspection and another perform any work, under the supervision of the first expert. The cost of having asbestos removed depends on the amount and its accessibility. You will have to pay extra for any sample you have analyzed by a laboratory.

Make sure that any contractor you hire isn't a fly-by-night outfit. The firm should have a permanent office and proper credentials.

Asbestos in the Home

Asbestos may be found everywhere in a house, from the basement to the roof, in houses 20 years old or older (See Figure 6-2.) Generally, the fibers present no danger if they are undamaged and locked in place.

1. Some roofing and siding shingles use a cement containing asbestos. (See Figure 6-3.)

2. Houses built between 1930 and 1950 may have asbestos as insulation.

Figure 6-2.   Asbestos roofing.

Figure 6-3.   Asbestos siding.

3. Asbestos may be presented in textured paint and in patching compounds used on wall and ceiling joints. Their use was banned in 1977.

4. Fireplace bricks and mortar may contain asbestos, and the flue may be lined with asbestos.

5. Older appliances such as toasters and refrigerators may have asbestos components, but they are considered fairly safe.

6. Wood-burning stoves may be insulated with asbestos paper, millboard, or cement sheets.

7. Asbestos may be found in some vinyl floor tiles.

8. Hot-water and steam pipes in older houses may be coated with an asbestos material or covered with an asbestos blanket or tape.

9. Oil and coal furnaces may have asbestos insulation.

Source: U.S. Consumer Product Safety Commission, U.S. Environmental Protection Agency.

Dealing with Asbestos

If you determine that there is asbestos in your home, keep these points in mind:

- Don't saw or drill tiles that may contain asbestos; don't let curtain rods, room dividers, or doors bump into ceilings that may contain asbestos; don't stack anything against asbestos-clad pipes.

- Lightly wet any area that may harbor asbestos fibers, and use a wet mop to clean up. Don't use a regular broom or a vacuum cleaner, which may disperse the particles into the air.

- Open windows in any area where asbestos may have been disturbed. Keep people and pets away. If the spill is large, call in an asbestos-abatement firm.

- Should you ever take it upon yourself to cover any material in your house that may contain asbestos? Most experts say no: You might disturb the asbestos. But a few experts suggest that if the asbestos material seems to be in good shape, you might coat it with latex paint. Latex paint may be safer to apply than duct tape or aluminum foil.

RADON

Real estate contracts commonly contain contingency clauses with regard to radon, calling upon the seller to reduce the radon level to an acceptable level before the closing, or calling for a certain amount of money to be set aside.

In some states, certain banks offer home-improvement loans just to remedy radon problems, at relatively low interest rates. Correcting a radon problem may cost from a few hundred to two thousand dollars.

An odorless, colorless gas, radon is created from the decay of the element uranium. People exposed to high indoor concentrations over long periods of time have a greater-than-normal risk of developing lung cancer.

The concentrations of radon in a building can vary tremendously from day to day and from season to season. Yet you won't notice. The gas doesn't irritate eyes, skin, or nose, and it has no immediate effect on breathing. Radon enters the body only through the lungs, and it can take from 5 to 50 years before someone develops a health problem.

Radon can permeate soil. It can enter buildings through openings in the foundation, through cracks in concrete floors and walls, and through floor drains, sump pumps, and hollow-block walls. It can also be drawn into a house where there is low air pressure, which may be caused by kitchen or attic exhaust fans, a warm indoor temperature, furnaces, clothes dryers, or other appliances that consume indoor air. In a house with a private well, radon can enter through faucets, shower heads, dishwashers, and clothes washers.

Radon levels are generally highest in the basement or ground level of a house. For a good idea of what the average levels in a home are, you can measure the levels over different seasons and in different areas.

Two of the most common devices to measure radon levels are the charcoal canister and the alpha-track canister. For the charcoal canister, you need a test period of three to seven days. For the alpha-track monitor, you need one to three months. A new, more dependable type of radon screening is the electret chamber. Continuous-level monitors are also available for reliable short-term and long-term radon testing.

A typical American house has about 1 picocurie of radon gas per liter (pCi/L) or about 0.005 working levels (WL) of radon decay products. If the average annual radon concentrations in your house exceed 4 pCi/L or 0.02 WL (the E.P.A.'s action level), you should take steps to reduce the levels. If the concentrations are greater than about 200 pCi/L or about 1 WL in a living area, you have a very serious problem.

If a test does indicate that a house contains a high level of radon, get in touch with your state's department of environmental protection, which may conduct further tests, free of charge to you.

The amount of danger that radon presents depends on:

- The average concentration of radon in the building;
- The number of years a person has lived in the building; and
- The amount of time the person spends there each day.

To deal with a radon problem, a homeowner should try to prevent it from entering the house and get rid of any that is already there ("mitigation"). (See Figure 6-4.) The steps may include sealing cracks and openings, covering exposed earth, and improving natural indoor ventilation.

Some other methods include:

- Forced ventilation—Fans and such can exchange the radon-contaminated air with outdoor air. (See Figure 6-4.)
- Heat-recovery ventilation—A heat exchanger uses the hot or cold air being ventilated to heat or cool the radon-free outdoor air that comes in.
- Block-wall ventilation—A solid horizontal duct is sealed in place over the horizontal wall-floor joints around the sides of the entire basement. The radon-contaminated air is then mechanically vented to the outside.

Figure 6-4.   Fan and piping to eliminate radon.

- Pressurization—The basement is sealed off from the rest of the house, and air from the upper floors is brought to the basement, increasing the gas pressure there and driving it outdoors.
- Sub-slab suction—Pipes are installed vertically into the foundation, to draw the radon-contaminated air from below the building to the outside. This is the most common residential radon-mitigation method. It costs about $1,500 for the average home. (See Figure 6-5.)

LEAD

Why is Lead Dangerous?

Lead is a metal found in rocks and soils. The poisonous effects of lead have been known since ancient times. Recent research shows

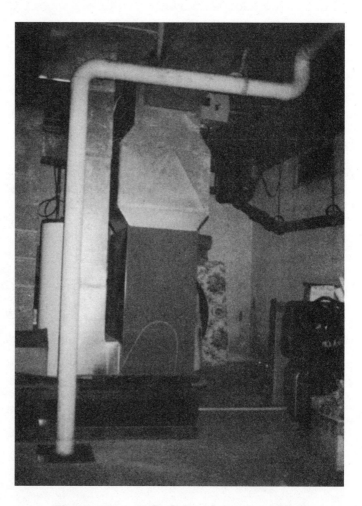

Figure 6-5.   Sub-slab radon mitigation.

that lead is a greater danger at lower levels of concentration than had been previously thought.

Airborne lead enters the body when someone breathes in lead particles or swallows lead dust. Until recently, the most important source of airborne dust was automobile exhausts.

When ingested, lead accumulates in the blood, bones, and soft tissue of the body. High concentrations can cause permanent damage to the central nervous system, the brain, the kidneys, and the red blood cells. Even low levels of lead may increase blood pressure in adults. But lead is more damaging to children because it's more easily absorbed into their bodies and their tissues are more vulnerable to its damaging effects. Very young children will eat flaking paint chips because it tastes sweet.

What are Sources of Lead in and Around the Home?

Lead can be in drinking water, in paint inside or outside a home, in the dust within a home, and in soil around the home.

How Does Lead Enter Drinking Water?

Water supply lines to many older houses were made of lead. Many homes built before 1988 contain plumbing systems that use lead-based solder in pipe connections. In such systems, lead can enter drinking water as a byproduct when plumbing fixtures, pipes, and solder are corroded by water. In 1988, Congress banned the use of lead-based solder in plumbing applications within homes and buildings.

How Widespread is Lead Paint in Houses?

Lead paint is very widespread, especially in old houses. According to the Environmental Protection Agency, lead-based paint was applied to about two-thirds of the houses built in the United States before 1940; to one-third of the houses from 1940 to 1960; and to a smaller percentage of houses built since 1960.

How Can I Tell Whether the Paint in a Home Contains Lead?

The only accurate ways to tell whether the paint in a home contains lead are to have a sample of the paint tested in a laboratory or to have an in-home test.

How Else Can Lead-based Paint be Harmful,
Besides Children Eating the Chips?

Lead can enter the air when surfaces covered with lead-based paint are scraped, sanded, or heated with an open flame when someone is paint-stripping. Lead particles freed in fine dust or vapors may settle into carpet fibers and fabric and be recirculated into the air by household cleaning. Fine particles penetrate the filter systems of home vacuum cleaners and are recirculated into the exhaust air streams of such appliances.

How Can I Get Rid of Lead-based Paint?

It's best to leave the paint undisturbed if it's in good condition and there's little chance that it will be eaten by children. Otherwise, you could cover it with special wallpaper or apply a sealant. Professional paint removal is costly and inconvenient. Consult with your state Department of Environmental Protection for specific local requirements and recommendations.

SAFE DRINKING WATER

You shouldn't have to "search the barren waste," as the old song goes, for the taste of cool, clean water. It should be as close as your household taps. If the house you're purchasing doesn't have any type of water treatment equipment, consider installing such equipment after you've moved in.

The first step in assuring good, safe water for your family is knowing what is already in your water.

If you're buying in a developed area, don't relax just because your water company regularly makes sure that its water supply meets Environmental Protection Agency standards. Much could happen to your water between the time the water leaves the water company's custody and when it reaches your tap. The underground piping to your house, the lead in your house piping, or even radon could be endangering your water quality. If you rely on a well, your risks are even greater.

In any case, have your water evaluated. Most laboratories will charge about $50 for a lead check, but self-test kits are available at hardware and home centers. Basic water analysis starts at $75 for bacteria and some contaminants. Ask your real estate agent for the names of local labs.

Here are the most effective and popular types of water protection devices:

- Activated carbon or charcoal filters—These devices remove general taste and odor problems, including chlorine residue. They can also help remove radon. They do not remove nitrates, bacteria, or metals like lead. The units can be installed at the sink (point of use) or on your house water supply (point of entry).

- Reverse osmosis systems—An RO unit commonly removes more than 90 percent of the total dissolved solids (including metals) and some organic chemicals, including most pesticides. It works by forcing water through a membrane having microscopic holes that allow water molecules, but not larger compounds, to pass through.

- Distillation units—These devices remove minerals such as nitrate, sodium, sulfate, and many organic chemicals. Distillation units remove virtually all impurities so that the water is mineral-free (and some say tasteless). They boil water, making steam, which is then condensed and collected as purified water.

- Water softeners—They make hard water soft by exchanging the minerals that cause hard water (calcium and magnesium) with sodium. Water softeners improve the cleaning action of soaps and detergents, and prevent scale buildup in pipes and equipment (like a hot-water heating system).

To evaluate your prospective home's present water treatment system, talk with officials at the installing company.

Red Flags

✔ Material that may contain asbestos is damaged.

✔ Repairs or renovations are being made, and they might disturb any "sleeping" asbestos.

✔ The owner has never tested the house for radon. (Even if he or she has, you should nonetheless do your own test.)

✔ Lead water pipes. Ask your local housing office for advice.

✔ Peeling paint—especially in older houses, which commonly contain lead-based paint.

✔ Clues that your drinking water may not be ideal: green-blue (copper) or brown (iron or manganese) staining on fixtures and in sinks; poor sudsing action (hard water); odors (like rotten eggs—hydrogen sulfide); fine sand (a well problem) in faucet strainers; leaky faucets (hard water); and strong tastes (as of chlorine).

7

FALLS AND FIRES

The most dangerous month, in terms of fatal accidents, is August. That's when more people are in the water and more people are on the highways. But eliminate car deaths and drownings, and December and January become the most dangerous months—and most of the fatal accidents during those months happen in and around people's homes.

In checking out a house before buying it, be on the lookout for dangerous steps, stairs, and stairways in particular. (See Figure 7-1.) The main reason homes can be so hazardous is simply that most have stairways. Every year, 2 million to 3 million Americans are disabled in falls; 800,000 of them must be hospitalized. And 85 percent of those accidents occur in homes. (See Table 7-1.)

Every year ten times as many Americans die in falls as drown. That's also twice as many as die in fires, and 8 times as many as are killed by firearms. Falls kill more Americans than any other kind of accident except for motor vehicles—and for Americans 55 and over, falls kill even more people than cars do.

STEPPING INTO AIR

The three key reasons why stairs are so dangerous, says life-safety specialist Jake Pauls, are:

- Most handrails next to stairways are virtually useless;
- The steps themselves are too narrow; and
- The lighting is inadequate.

Although 80 percent of the accident-related deaths involve the elderly, the injuries occur among all age groups, adds Pauls, who is

Figure 7-1.   Sunken front walk.

with Hughes Associates, an engineering consulting firm in Wheaton, Maryland.

Even a small tumble can be dangerous. "You don't have to fall down many steps to have a serious injury," Pauls says. "Even with a few steps you could fall ten feet in a tumbling fall."

Basement steps may be the biggest threat. The stairs there, he says, are the most likely to be of lower quality and poorly lighted.

Many houses with stairs don't even have handrails. If they do, the rails may not be "grabbable": They may be mainly for decoration, and so large that you can't get your fingers and thumb fully around them. They may also be too low. They should be 36 inches above the "nosing" (the front of a step), whereas many are only 30 to 32 inches above. Get a ruler, and measure the distances in any house you're considering buying.

Even children need high handrails, Pauls insists. The higher the hold, the more effective the rail is for helping you retain your posture. For adults, handrails should be hip or elbow height; for children, head height.

"Overstepping"—stepping into the air instead of onto a stair—is the most common cause of falls. The chief reason: the steps or treads are too short. To provide a good foothold, the steps should be about 12 inches long. Most are about 9 inches long. Building codes permit 9-inch treads, and if you have carpeting you could lose another ½

How People Die in Home Accidents			
Type of Accident	1989 Death Toll *	% Change from 1988	Death Rate
Falls	6,600	3	2.7%
Poisoning (solids, liquids)	4,700	12	1.9
Fires, burns	3,300	-13	1.3
Suffocation (ingested object)	2,700	-4	1.1
Others**	2,400	-8	1.0
Firearms	900	0	0.4
Suffocation (mechanical)***	700	40	0.3
Poisoning (gas, vapors)	600	0	0.2
Drowning	600	-14	0.2

*Per 100,000 population.
**Includes electric current, explosive materials, hot substances, corrosive liquids, and steam.
***Includes smothering by bed clothes, plastic materials, and so on.
Source: National Safety Council.

Table 7.1

inch to 1 inch. Treads are measured from (1) the beginning of the overhang of the tread above to (2) the nosing, minus the rounded carpet part that doesn't provide support.

The treads themselves should be neutral in color and not have geometric designs, which may act as camouflage in concealing the nosing. Ideally, the nosing should be easy to see, which is why stairs in public places may have yellow paint on the tread edges.

The lighting on stairs should be from the bottom up, not from the top down, or you will walk into pools of dark. Three out of four serious falls occur when people walk down stairs, not up. But the light downstairs shouldn't be so bright as to blind you.

RUGS AND CARPETS

Scatter rugs are another common cause of falls. People don't actually slip on them; they stumble on them. This is especially the case with older people, who don't lift their legs as high as younger people do.

The conventional advice is that scatter rugs should have rubber mats underneath. Pauls argues that these mats make scatter rugs even worse. "Just throw out any scatter rugs," he advises.

Carpeting is a different story. If it's not worn, it can act as buffer if someone falls. With a carpet, says Nina Moroz, program manager for home and recreational safety at the National Safety Council, you may wind up with a bruise instead of a break.

PREVENTING FIRES

The obvious reason for the December–January surge in fatalities is that more people are indoors then, because of the holidays and because of the cold weather. Another reason is the greater danger of fires. Home heating systems are in full use then, and more electricity in general is consumed on such things as Christmas trees and holiday lighting. In December and January, many more Americans die in fires than in other months.

Some precautions for homebuyers:

- Look for the Underwriters Laboratories seal on all lighting, and check wires for fraying. With outside lighting, make sure the wires aren't wedged under aluminum siding or into nails, which could act as conductors.

Figure 7-2.   Ceiling smoke detector.

The Most Dangerous Consumer Products	
Product	*Injuries*
Stairs, ramps, landings, floors	1,477,887
Cutlery, knives (unpowered)	337,464
Beds, mattresses, pillows	299,222
Chairs, sofas, beds	291,446
Tables	269,255
Nails, carpettacks, etc.	220,640
Playground equipment	204,726
Ceilings, walls, panels	186,328
Cans, other containers	183,023
Glass doors, windows, panels	176,393
Source: National Safety Council.	

- If the house has a second floor, there should be a portable ladder up there.
- Smoke detectors can be a blessing, but most homes don't have enough. One on each floor should be the minimum. Good places are outside bedrooms, at the tops of stairs, and in hallways. A bad place is in a kitchen, where a smoke detector can go off all too readily when there's no fire. (See Figure 7-2.)

For further advice, see Chapter 24, "Electrical Systems."

Red Flags

- ✔ Stairs and stairways that are dangerous—because the handrails are virtually useless, the steps themselves are too narrow, the lighting is inadequate, or the steps are too short.
- ✔ No Underwriters Laboratories seals on all lighting.
- ✔ Frayed wires.
- ✔ Wires for lighting that are wedged under aluminum siding or into nails.
- ✔ Electrical problems—from aluminum wiring to inadequate wattage.
- ✔ Nonworking smoke detectors (spent battery-powered units or unconnected electric units).

IV

OUTSIDE THE HOUSE

8

BUYING THE NEIGHBORHOOD

Many people decide to buy a house because it reminds them of where their grandparents lived, or because their furniture will fit nicely into the rooms, or because there's a view of a lake. Only after they buy do they learn about the high property taxes or discover that the area is deteriorating and so are property values.

Choosing a good community should be one of the chief goals of house hunters. Yet all too many people make horrendous mistakes, such as buying mainly for emotional or trivial reasons.

THE GOOD COMMUNITY

By definition, says James Hughes, professor of urban planning at Rutgers University, a desirable community is a place where:

- Your house should appreciate over the years;
- You'll enjoy efficient services (fire, police, garbage collection, libraries); and
- You will have a top-notch school system, a variety of social activities available, and friendly, helpful neighbors.

The worst mistake may be putting the cart before the horse. "Buying the house instead of the community is the biggest mistake people make," says Chris Siepert, manager of corporate services for Relocation 1 in Fairfield, New Jersey, part of Coldwell Banker Realtors. "People should shop the town before they shop the house."

Another mistake is choosing an area mainly because of possible price appreciation. This usually means a community with a glamorous name—Beverly Hills, Greenwich, Princeton, Grosse Pointe. Homes in these elite communities do tend to hold their property values better. "The primary markets—Princeton, Greenwich, Ridgewood—are the last where houses lose their value in a slump and the first to come back in a revival," says Michael T. Robinson, president of Weichert Relocation in Morris Plains.

Still, buying a house in Upper Crust can be a mistake if you can't afford it or if the lifestyle isn't your lifestyle. If you go unshaven on weekends or don't believe in dressing to the nines on your days off, Top shelf may not be your cup of beer.

Many people take on too much when they opt for glamorous communities. Just to afford the house, they may have to deny themselves almost everything else. "They have a bedroom set, living room furniture, and not much else," says Wilbur Heinemeyer, an appraiser. "They're house-poor—just keeping their heads above water."

One reason some job transferees buy into their ultra-expensive communities is that their new coworkers strongly recommend these towns. Yet "The worst advice you can get comes from your coworkers," argues John G. Rolwell, president of the Relocation Group Inc. in Hackensack. "Typically, a transferee's coworkers know only one community. And if someone's boss says, 'I live in Saddle River,' this poor guy may not remember that he gets only half his boss's salary."

Besides which, the snobbish atmosphere of certain communities may not appeal to the average Joe and Jane. Siepert recalls a Southern family that fell in love with a posh Northern community simply because they liked its looks. After living there a while, the wife felt ostracized and took to her bed. Their young son was ridiculed by schoolmates because of his accent. They eventually moved back down South.

If parents can barely scrape enough money together to buy a house in Upper Crust, they may not have anything left to buy their kids the designer clothes and snappy styles other youngsters have, says Carolyn Weber, vice president of regional development for Century 21 in New York City. The parents themselves might not be able to afford the country club to which most of their neighbors belong.

Then too, houses in a blue-chip town cost far more than comparable houses in other communities. A house in Darien identical to one in Fairfield might cost two or even three times as much. "Elite communities have great amenities and social packages, but you pay a high price," says Hughes. "The actual shelter you buy may be mediocre—not nearly as nice as you could buy elsewhere." In any case, even houses in Upper Crust don't come with warranties. "There are no guaranteed winners," Hughes says.

A good compromise for people who cannot afford Upper Crust or might not care for its stuck-up lifestyle is to buy in a nearby town. Just basking in the glow of Upper Crust helps keep a satellite community's property values high. Hughes gives an example: "West Windsor is less prestigious than Princeton, but the schools there are just as good—and the houses are lower-priced."

In any case, homebuyers shouldn't simply concentrate on the possible profits they might make from their houses. "It's okay if your house doesn't make money," says Hughes, "so long as you don't actually lose money. The question is: What kind of house and community do you want? Do you think you will be happy living there for ten years?"

To choose the best place for yourself and your family, you should (1) determine exactly what you want and (2) do some detective work. Draw up a list of your needs and desires—and ask yourself whether a community you have in mind will satisfy them. "Ideally," says Weber, "people should move to places that change their lifestyles the least. Otherwise, you may not be relocated so much as dislocated."

Do you want lots of land and privacy or a reasonably sized plot, along with a small town atmosphere? Do you want public sewers and public water or a rural atmosphere?

Are you eager to have good schools and a short commute (typical of younger people) or good health-care facilities? Do you want a place to swim, golf, or bicycle? Do you want shopping within walking distance, or would you mind having to get into your car to pick up a bottle of milk?

If a new community is deficient in one respect, maybe there are trade-offs. You might be willing to commute for a half-hour every day in return for a four-bedroom house instead of a three-bedroom, or for a school system with classes for gifted children.

You can tell a lot about a town just by looking around. Are the streets clean? Are residents well-to-do enough so that houses don't need paint and lawns don't need reseeding? Are people repairing their own cars in their driveways? Are homeowners prohibited from keeping trucks or boats in their yards? Are business areas clearly separated from residential areas?

Is the community diversified? Is there a mix of architectural styles, from ranches to colonials to tudors? Are there new houses as well as older ones? Are there young homeowners (who may vote for school budgets) as well as old homeowners (who may vote against school budgets, yet who serve to keep the schools from being overcrowded)?

A school system's reputation can hardly be overestimated. It's the main reason many people choose a particular town. Because it's so hard for a layperson to evaluate a school system, a school's reputation may be more important than the true quality of the schools. But Hughes suspects that reputation and reality shouldn't be far apart.

One way to evaluate a school is to check with School Match, a data-based information and counseling service in Westerville, Ohio. The telephone number is 1-800-992-5323. The cost of a list of suitable schools, after you answer a questionnaire, is $97.50. The cost of learning how your school stacks up against others is $49.

Another way to evaluate a community is to study its effective tax rate. But a mistake many buyers make is assuming that high taxes themselves are undesirable. The question is whether the tax money is being squandered or whether it's paying for good services like clean, well-maintained streets, a high-quality school system, a library, police and fire protection, and refuse collection.

Be certain to visit the local municipal offices and talk to the people in the building inspection/code enforcement departments. Inquire about community concerns such as flood zones, toxic sites, planned highways/roads, septic and water problems, and so on. Find out if your prospective home or neighborhood has a history of health or other violations.

WHY BUYERS BUY WHERE THEY DO

What homebuyers want in a community depends to a large extent upon their ages. The elderly, for example, may be seeking good health-care facilities, a warm climate, and closeness to friends and family. But in general buyers want an affordable house in a good neighborhood.

In a 1988 survey by the National Association of Realtors, 662 buyers said they chose their home because it was:

Within their price range	87%
In a better neighborhood	71
Near good schools	53
Near their place of work	48
Near a shopping area	47
Near parks, recreation	41
Near family, friends	37
Near good transportation	30
Near health and public services	29
A good provider of rental income	11

Red Flags

✔ The house is far better than the street it's on.

✔ You might be able to afford the house but not the lifestyle.

✔ The house and community are fine, but not quite right for you
   and your family. You swim and play golf and like an old, rural
   area; the community caters to theater lovers and tennis play-
   ers, and it's new and citified.

✔ You want top-notch schools, and the reputation of the local
   system is mixed. And on a number of tests, the school system
   flunks—expenditures per pupil, size of classrooms, percentage of youngsters who proceed to college.

✔ Major drawbacks (airport, busy roads, toxic waste sites, etc.).

9

FROM COLONIALS TO CONTEMPORARIES: HOUSE STYLES

Which is the ugliest house style? The most inefficient type of house? Is it a sin for a homeowner to install aluminum siding on a Colonial?

Although such questions don't have definitive answers, it's not hard to find people espousing passionate points of view. House styles can arouse powerful emotions.

In fact, where many homebuyers go wrong is being too emotional—paying too much attention to a house's appearance and not enough to its practicality. So they may overextend themselves by purchasing sprawling ranches, for example, which may be costly to build, to buy, and to maintain—sort of the high-priced spread. Or they may opt for striking Tudors, which also can be wickedly expensive.

If there's one valid generalization about house styles, it's that one-story homes are more suitable for wealthy older people, whereas one-and-a-half or two-story houses are better for not-so-wealthy young people. (See Figures 9-1 through 9-8.)

Of course, all styles have advantages and drawbacks, just as all house types do, whether they be one-story or three.

One-story houses—typically, **ranch** houses—are easy to clean and maintain. You need not lug a vacuum cleaner up and down stairs, you can climb up on the roof to remove leaves from the gutters, and you can paint the house yourself without climbing on a tall ladder. You don't have to climb stairs all the time.

But ranches make inefficient use of land, which is why areas where land is scarce, as in the Northeast, have few single-story houses. And

Ranch

This style of house features one-level living. There may be a full or partial basement. Generally, a garage is attached to the side of the house. The major advantage is step-saving convenience. Ranch houses are usually more expensive to build than colonials or split levels. But they are often easier to maintain than a multi-level house. There are many different floor plans to satisfy almost every desire. The most popular style is the straight side-to-side ranch.

Split Level

This style of house became very popular following WWII because of the amount of space and utility provided. Split levels fall into two types: side-to-side and front-to-back. Many split level houses have a basement. The next level, usually at ground level, contains a den/playroom. The next levels contain the kitchen/dining room/living room and the bedrooms/bathrooms. The attic area offers another level and often can be expanded for additional space in the future.

Price Range: _____

Comments: _____

_____

_____

Figure 9-1.   Ranch house.

Figure 9-2.   Split-level.

not only do ranches call for more land; you also need more excavation, longer walls, longer mechanical systems, and a bigger roof.

Heating and cooling costs are higher in a ranch because heat escapes through the roof, and if you have twice the roof size, you have twice the heat loss. You'll also have to pay a king's ransom if you ever must replace the roof.

One architect admits that he is biased against ranches. "It offends me to have an entire house on one floor," he grouses. "It's an extravagance. Unless someone has a health problem, I think that a two-story is as livable as a one-story."

Yet ranches have their admirers. "Ranches are by far the most popular houses in this country," reports Henry S. Harrison, an appraiser and broker in New Haven, Connecticut. "Some people feel that one-story living is great—and anyone who runs up and down the stairs in a two-story house six times a day is nuts."

Two-story houses—typically, **Colonials**—are often less expensive than one-stories. They're sort of a box built on a box, so they're cheaper to build, cheaper to heat, and cheaper to cool. Another benefit of a two-story house is that the sleeping areas are far away

Colonial

This style of two story house has been a mainstay of U.S. architecture for many years. These are generally quality built houses — many were custom built. The main appeal seems to be the spaciousness and elegance. There are many variations of colonial style houses available. The colonial house built in the past 30 years may consist of a partially finished basement, a first floor with a living room, dining room, eat-in kitchen, family room, porch and powder room. The second floor contains the bedrooms and bathrooms.

Price Range: _____

Comments: _____
_____
_____

Cape Cod

This very practical one and one-half story style of house has been popular for many years, with most capes concentrated in the northeastern portion of the U.S. In the past forty years, hundreds of thousands of cape cods have been built. Many resale capes have been expanded over the years for increased living area. Standard cape cods have a first floor kitchen, living room, dining room, bathroom and a bedroom. The second floor contains one or two small bedrooms. Capes are space-efficient and have maintained their value over the years.

Price Range: _____

Comments: _____
_____
_____

Figure 9-3.   Colonial.   **Figure 9-4.   Cape Cod.**

from the living areas, so parents can party downstairs while their children snooze upstairs.

A blatant drawback of two-story houses, of course, is that you must forever climb up and down stairs. One solution: installing a master bedroom on the first floor. And then there is the danger of your being caught on the second floor in a fire. Still, new construction requires that second-floor windows be large enough for people to escape from. And smoke alarms have become ubiquitous.

Cape Cods, which provide one-and-a-half stories, are, like Colonials, also suitable for young homeowners. They're inexpensve, too, because part of the roof serves as walls and because they also use space efficiently.

As a family grows, a Cape Cod can be expanded: The attic can be turned into living quarters. But once an attic is finished, it can be tricky and expensive to provide new insulation—by putting material under the rafters or under the outside shingles. The cost of extra insulation should be reflected in the asking price.

Bi-levels and **split levels** are also economical, in part because you need not spring for the cost of a true basement. In effect, such houses have lifted the basement out of the ground.

But splits and bilevels may be difficult to heat evenly: The upper floors may be too warm, the lower floors too cool. And, of course, you have all that stair-climbing.

Bi-levels have fewer levels than splits, and this may explain their greater popularity. But these days builders tend to ignore both types. Still, on a sloping lot, bi-levels can be ideal. Two main floors can have direct access to the outdoors.

While splits have fallen out of favor, **Victorians**, with their multitude of rooms, ornate decorations, and flowery woodwork, are staging a comeback. "They have a richness of visual interest and color," notes one architect. A drawback: If you need repairs, you will find good repairpeople hard to find. Repainting a Victorian will also be expensive, and so will insurance to replace the gingerbread trim in case of a fire.

As for what most people call **Tudors**, they should more aptly be called Elizabethans. Real Tudors have few half-timbers in their

Contemporary

These "casual" houses are usually sheathed in redwood or stained hardwood and come in many sizes and shapes. Usually found in resort or second-home development areas, contemporary style houses are becoming more evident in typical suburban areas. The most familiar and popular contemporary style house is the A frame. These houses are designed to fit into a rustic landscape. Many times, this style features cathedral ceilings, large expanse of glass and decks surrounding one to three sides of the house.

Price Range: _____

Comments: _____
_____
_____

Figure 9-5.   Contemporary.

Bi-Level

This style of house is also referred to as a split ranch. The bi-level house is a modified version of the ranch house, with the major difference being that the lower level is more out of the ground than in the ground. Seldom is there a basement. Entry is often to the center of the house, with the foyer being split between the lower and upper levels. The lower area will frequently consist of a built-in garage and a storage area. Many bi-levels are featured in housing developments throughout the U.S., and most were built after 1950.

Price Range: _____

Comments: _____
_____
_____

Figure 9-6.   Bi-level.

Victorian

The victorian style of house was built in various models during the turn of the last century. Home buyers appreciate the architectural nuances of victorian houses including large porches and interesting bay windows. As with most older houses, conditions and selling prices vary greatly. Those which have been mechanically updated through the years and have been well maintained may command premium prices, while those which have received less annual attention often offer classic charm at reasonable prices.

Price Range: _____

Comments: _____

_____

_____

Figure 9-7.   Victorian.

Townhouse

This style of house takes its name from the type of house which dominated the early residential development of our major cities, notably the row houses. The townhouse, often sold in condominium developments, is an independent structure, usually of two or three stories, attached to another similar building on either one or two sides. Townhouse sizes normally vary in width from 16 to 24 feet. This style of house is usually economical to purchase and low in maintenance and utility costs.

Price Range: _____

Comments: _____

_____

_____

Figure 9-8.   Townhouse.

walls. But whether they're called Tudors or Elizabethans, they have, as one broker puts it, a lot of pizzazz.

But Tudors aren't for people of modest means. Authentic Tudors, with their half-buried timbers, stucco walls, leaded-glass windows, complicated roofs, and two to two-and-a-half stories, are expensive. And although their slate roofs last almost forever, the roof valleys are subject to leaks. Some homeowners also complain that builders, in striving for authenticity, make the inside of Tudors too dark.

Unfortunately, not enough builders seem to strive for authenticity. Inauthentic Tudors abound, and these, with their prefinished stucco board and ordinary boards instead of half-timbers, are the ugliest type of house, says one architect. "They look cheap and they are cheap."

The question of authenticity in general arouses strong feelings among architects. One of them believes that architects and builders should respect authentic styles more. Yet he accepts aluminum siding and vinyl-clad windows on traditional house styles like Colonials. "New materials are a fact of life," he says.

The style of a house helps determine its weaknesses and strengths. When the roof on a one-story house goes, for example, the expense

Tudor

Tudors and other English style houses were built in the U.S. during the period of the late 1800's through the 1920's. The combination of stucco and distinctive wood trim exterior provides the tudor style house with a uniqueness which is most appealing. Tudors are also noted for their gables, large angular chimneys and slate roofs. Tudors are particularly appealing to families with large space needs. Like the victorian, the condition of a tudor will vary greatly depending upon its upgrading and maintenance over the years.

Price Range: _____

Comments: _____

_____

_____

Figure 9-9.   Tudor.

will be far more than with a two-story house, simply because the roof is so much bigger. The nooks and crannies of a Tudor may make the second-story rooms somewhat dark. A Cape Cod may be too hot in summer and too cold in winter, if the top floor is converted into bedrooms instead of being used as insulation.

Here are the main styles of houses and their typical attributes:

- Ranch—One story. Requires a large lot, large foundation, large roof and long walls. Costly to build and costly to heat and cool. Hardly any stair-climbing. Easy to clean inside and repair outside. Adaptable to outdoors living.

- Colonials—Two stories. Good for young families, because the sleeping areas are far from the recreational rooms, but older homeowners may not enjoy the incessant stair-climbing. Heating and cooling costs are lower than with a one-story. Fairly inexpensive to build: You don't need a big foundation or roof. The second floor can be a dangerous place to be in case of a fire.

- Cape Cod—One-and-a-half stories. If the attic is finished, the house may become too hot in summer and too cold in winter.

The rooms upstairs may be small, with small windows. But heating costs should be low, and so should the price of the house. Such houses are concentrated in the Northeast.

- Bi-level—Also referred to as a split ranch. Entry is usually in a central foyer, which is split between two levels. Space use is very efficient. A bi-level is well suited to a sloping lot.

- Split level—The living area is on the entry level. You walk down to the social area and up to the sleeping area. Lots of stair-climbing. Bedrooms may be too warm. A good design for a slanted lot.

- Victorian—Large porches, interesting bay windows, rich architectural details. Conditions and selling prices vary enormously inasmuch as these are older houses.

- Tudor—Two or two-and-a-half stories. Stucco or stone walls, with half timbers imbedded in them. Because of roof angles, leaks are more likely. House is hard to heat evenly. Second-floor rooms may be dark. But the slate roof lasts almost forever, and the house's appearance is striking. Also called an Elizabethan.

- Townhouse—An independent structure, usually two to three stories, attached to another similar building on one or two sides. Sizes vary in width from 16 to 24 feet. Because of the shared walls, townhouses are usually economical to buy and maintain. Often sold in condominium developments.

- Contemporary—"Casual" houses, usually sheathed in redwood or stained hardwood. A-frames are the most popular. Designed to fit into a rustic landscape. Features cathedral ceiling, large expanses of glass, and decks surrounding one to three sides of the house.

Red Flags

✔ The house is a knock-out—a striking Tudor, for example. But the house inspector, after checking the heating system, the electrical system, the plumbing system, the roof, the basement, and so forth is decidedly unimpressed. And you're kidding yourself along by thinking, "Well, so I have to spend a little on repairs..."

✔ You hate climbing stairs, yet you've fallen in love with a charming Colonial or Split-level.

✔ You're not sure what style a house is, or what the style's advantages or disadvantages are, yet you're ready to put in a bid.

✔ A house is so unusual, there may not be a ready buyer when you want to sell.

10

OUTSIDE WALLS

The outside walls of a house are usually made of masonry, wood, vinyl, or aluminum.

The best skin for a house, in many ways, is masonry (brick or stone). It will need less care than wood. It's fire-resistant, though not fire-proof, and will outlast most other sidings. On the other hand, the mortar between bricks or stones may need repointing (upgrading) over the years. You can test it with a penknife to check whether it's become soft and porous. (See Figure 10-1.) Masonry, by the way, isn't as good an insulator as you may think. Wood is better.

Another concern with masonry is efflorescence—the deposit of a chalky powder from the minerals that leech out with moisture. It's most noticeable on the walls of damp or wet basements, and while it's bothersome, it's not serious. You can clean it off with a stiff brush and muriatic acid.

Wood framing may be shingles, shakes, horizontal or vertical clapboards, or large panels. Shingles are machine-cut, not split; shakes are more rough-hewed and last longer. Check shingles or shakes for warping or cupping from moisture (and lack of care). (See Figure 10-2.)

Wood siding needs staining or painting every few years. Check the finish for peeling and blistering. If the house needs repainting frequently, you probably have a moisture problem. And if the paint is in such sorry shape that all of it must be removed, you're talking big bucks. The preparation expense will probably exceed the staining or painting expense.

Sight across the house to check how straight the sides are. Bulging walls are symptomatic of an underlying structural problem. Poke the wood closest to the ground with a screwdriver, to make sure it isn't the victim of termites or dry rot.

Figure 10-1.   Brick siding.

Figure 10-2.   Wood siding in poor condition.

Aluminum or vinyl siding should be snug. It should have a solid backing; watch out for any waviness. Quality aluminum or vinyl siding is guaranteed by the manufacturer against defects for 15 years or longer. Lesser-quality siding and siding that is not power-cleaned every five years may require painting (believe it or not). (See Figure 10-3.)

A drawback of retro-siding is that buyers may worry whether all the wood underneath has decayed. (If you push in the siding a few feet above the ground, you should be able to feel how hard the wood underneath is.)

Inspect the caulking around windows, doors, and trim. Is it doing its job of insulating and protecting against water penetration? Check the side of the house exposed to the worst weather. Also, worry about any ivy or vines growing on the house: Uncontrolled growth can cause damage—either directly or just by keeping out sunlight.

Cracks in any walls scare buyers, but most cracks are inconsequential and of no structural concern. Most cracks are vertical or "step" cracks (following the mortar joints in cement blocks). These are usually normal settlement cracks, which occur as the house settles on its foundation. Horizontal cracks, on the other hand, should be evaluated to determine the cause. These cracks are caused by exterior forces. In any case, any crack that is greater than a pencil width should be checked out, especially cracks wider at the top rather than

Figure 10-3.   Vinyl siding.

Figure 10-4.   Vertical settlement cracks.

at the bottom (V-cracks). They're usually a sign of settlement problems. (See Figure 10-4.)

Red Flags

✔ Shingles or shakes that are warped or cupped.

✔ Masonry with signs of neglect.

✔ Wood siding with blistering or peeling paint. If the paint must be removed, it's a gigantic expense.

✔ Bulging walls or uneven walls.

✔ If the wood close to the ground is soft, it may have been the victim of termites or dry rot.

✔ Waviness in aluminum or vinyl siding.

✔ You push against aluminum siding a few feet above the ground, and it gives.

✔ Vines or ivy have harmed the walls, by pulling away the siding, for example.

✔ You spot horizontal cracks in walls, larger than a pencil and wider on the top than on the bottom.

✔ Brick veneer pulling away from the house.

✔ Composition-wood siding that is swollen or soft, especially around nails or cut lines.

11

THE GREAT OUTDOORS

Examine the outside of a house (the grounds, the driveway, and so forth) in the daytime. You may conclude, despite what the sellers told you, that the charming little pond in the front yard is really an algae lagoon. (See Figure 11-1.)

In examining a house's grounds, study the lay of the land. Water should drain away from the house. The ground right next to the house should be graded away from the foundation—a slant of about 15 degrees (six inches for the first three feet); this will help divert surface water away from the house. Most wet basements are caused by roof or surface water that is not directed away from the foundation. Water from gutters and sump pumps should be drained to the street or to drywells on the property—underground containers of stones, where the water will be dispersed.

There shouldn't be sudden declines on the remainder of the grounds. A clue to a precipitous slope is bare earth, where the grass has been eroded away. If a property is at the bottom of a hill, obviously you should worry more about water problems than if it's at the top of a hill.

Sometimes it's hard to tell what might happen to a property after a heavy rain. That's why it's a splendid idea to visit a house you're interested in when it's raining or after a heavy rainfall. Puddles and pools are discouraging signs (especially if you find them indoors!). See if the roof and surface water flow is away from the house.

A broad lot is generally better than a narrow lot, simply because a wide house is more attractive. A regularly shaped lot is preferable to one that's irregular, if only because it will be easier to sell later on. A huge front lawn can help reduce street noise and impress visitors. Still, a big, private rear yard is better, although lawn mowing tends to lose its appeal after an hour or so.

Figure 11-1.   Pond in front yard.

If a survey is available, study it. Make sure the property lines are accurate and that no neighbors have built a shed or are storing firewood on what was once your property. (After a certain number of years, you can lose the right to property through "adverse possession" if other people regularly and openly use it as if it were theirs.) Also see if there are rights-of-way, allowing someone else to cross over your property.

Check the grass, flowers, and bushes. Keep in mind that if the grounds are as flowery and lush as the Garden of Eden, you (or a gardener you hire) will have a lot of work to do. Also remember that if the lawn has a sizable hill or steep decline, your lawn mowing may be tiring.

Check any trees. Can you tell if they're alive? Are there any sizable dead branches, which might fall on the house, garage, or electrical wires? Do the trees shed their leaves in winter, and how will that change your views? Might you see green leaves in summer and dark smokestacks in the winter? (Evergreens can protect your house from wind in winter.) Are big trees so near your house that their roots might cause problems? (They should be at least 10 feet away.) Weeping willows and poplars drink a lot of water, and their roots could be especially troublesome because they are shallow and spread over a wide area.

Inspect any fences, gates, walls, patios, sidewalks, decks, and outbuildings. Are they in good shape? If a gate doesn't swing smoothly, it may be trivial, but it could be a clue that the homeowner is generally neglectful. Find out who is responsible for a fence separating your property from your neighbor's and who prunes and otherwise maintains bushes dividing properties. Can the owners produce evidence that whoever built the deck obtained a building permit? (If it was constructed improperly, the moorings might pop out of the ground in freezing weather, or the untreated wood might decay in a few years instead of 40 years.) (See Figure 11-2.)

A patio should slope slightly away from the house; if it's covered with a carpet or artificial grass, check underneath for bad cracks.

A driveway that slopes toward the house may be a problem. Even if there's a drain next to the garage, it may clog up and let water pour in. A concrete driveway is generally better than asphalt; asphalt is generally better than pebbles, gravel, or dirt. Be on the lookout for cracks in any driveway—wide ones, not narrow ones.

When you are pulling out of the driveway, can you see down both sides of the street clearly? Is the traffic so heavy that you're taking your life in your hands whenever you pull out? Is the driveway long enough so it can accommodate several cars? (This is important in an area where there's no parking on the street overnight and you have

Figure 11-2.   Backyard deck.

Figure 11-3.   Long, steep driveway to house.

occasional guests.) But is the driveway not so long and steep that you may have problems if wintertime is snow time? (See Figure 11-3.)

Is there outdoor lighting? That can make outdoor dining a possibility and help discourage burglars. Are there outdoor electrical outlets for your barbecue and faucets for washing your car? Is there a garbage bin, or might dogs, cats, and other less savory things make a mess of your garbage?

If there's an aboveground pool, check the liner and sides for damage. If the pool is an in-the-ground type, have it and its equipment inspected. Is there a protective fence around any pool? If there's a tennis court, check the ground for smoothness and the fences for rust. A metal post that's directly in the ground will rust away faster than a post implanted into concrete.

Red Flags

- ✔ After a rainfall, you see lingering puddles.
- ✔ The property is graded toward the house.
- ✔ The yard has bare earth where water may have eroded away the ground.
- ✔ The driveway slopes toward the house or garage.
- ✔ The neighbors may be using some of your property (for example, they store firewood there).
- ✔ While you're pulling your car out of the driveway, you can't see up and down the street (perhaps a tree blocks your view).
- ✔ An aboveground pool's liner and sides are ripped; an in-ground pool hasn't passed a professional's inspection.

12

ROOFS, GUTTERS,
AND LEADERS

When people talk about a house, any house, they talk about having
"a roof over their heads." That's symbolic of how important a roof is
for the occupants of a house—for keeping rain and snow and sun
away and for keeping heat in.

Your first steps in inspecting a roof should be to check that the lines
of the peaks and valleys are straight and that there's no sagging. (See
Figure 12-1.) The chimney should soar straight up, not at an angle.

Using binoculars, check that the roofing materials are in good
shape. The southern and southwestern section, more vulnerable to
sunlight, may be in the worst condition. Look for signs of patching,
strong evidence that the roof has been leaking.

ASPHALT SHINGLES

Asphalt shingles, the most common roof covering, should be flat, not
curled; they should have plenty of the original mineral granules on
them, and not be cracked or broken. Also, their color shouldn't vary,
which means that the homeowner has been replacing them. (See
Figure 12-2.) You can test an asphalt shingle by bending the edge: It
should bend, and not break, meaning it still has oil and life to it.

Inspect the flashing, the thin metal around the chimney, dormers,
and other angled sections of the roof. It shouldn't have lifted, be
cracked, or have holes. (See Figure 12-3.)

If the gutters are filled with mineral granules that have come off
the shingles, it's another sign that the shingles are near the end of
their lives.

Figure 12-1.   Sagging garage roof.

Figure 12-2.   Patched asphalt shingles.

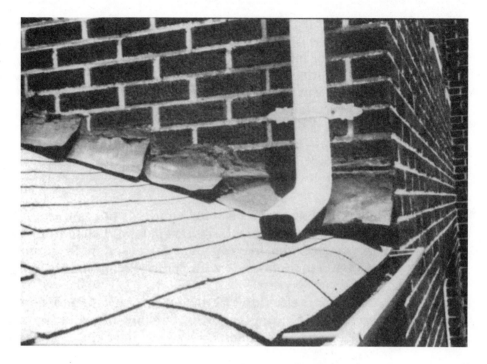

Figure 12-3.   Lifted roof flashings.

Beware of a roof that has a second layer of shingles over the first. Before a new third layer can be applied, the old shingles must be removed—an expensive project. You can tell whether the shingles are single layer or double by looking at them directly from the side: If there's a layer on bottom, the top shingle may become distorted—it will bulge or be depressed.

WOOD SHINGLES

About 10 percent of the residential roofs in this country are covered with wood—shingles or shakes. Almost all wood roofs are made from red cedar.

Shingles, which are less expensive, are sawn to a uniform shape. With care, they have a life span of 15 to 20 years. Their more expensive cousins, shakes, are thicker and are often handsplit rather than sawn. They generally last longer.

Both wood shingles and shakes come in varying grades, depending on the quality and thickness of the product. Ideally, both shingles and shakes should have been treated with a fire retardant.

On wood roofs, the flashing requires special attention because the acid in wood can corrode metal flashings, causing leaks.

Wood shingles and shakes shouldn't be cracked, thin, or rotted away; those on the shady side of a house in particular should be checked for mold.

Maintaining proper ventilation in an attic will boost the life expectancy of any wood roof. Applying a wood preservative to wood roofs every few years will reduce the drying effects of the sun and minimize the buildup of mold or moss.

SLATE

Slate roofs have been used for hundreds of years around the world. Most slate roofs have a long life span, and slate from Vermont and Virginia lasts the longest (over 50 years) with annual care. The service life of roofs made with Pennsylvania slate is in the moderate range (over 35 years).

Slate roofs shouldn't be flaked or cracked, and slates shouldn't be missing. Finding someone capable of replacing slate can be difficult; finding someone who will do it cheap almost requires a miracle.

A sagging slate roof is very worrisome: Slate roofs are heavy, and perhaps the house simply cannot sustain the weight. Rusting nails are also worrisome. The slates actually hang on these nails. Copper nails are better than galvanized nails because they last longer.

CLAY AND CONCRETE TILES

The classic red clay tile has been the mainstay of quality homes thoughout the South. Clay tiles are available in many shapes, from the traditional half barrel to flat types resembling wood shingles. Although unglazed clay tiles are porous and retain moisture, they have an expected life span of over 40 years if maintained properly.

In areas of high humidity, clay tiles should be pressure-cleaned to minimize darkening caused by mold or mildew. If unchecked, this condition will spoil the appearance of the tiles and shorten their life. Like slate, clay tiles weather well but are prone to breakage. As with slate, many roofers are unfamiliar with clay tile and will recommend replacing rather than repairing it.

Concrete roof tiles have become popular in the warm climates of the country. Made of cement, sand, and water, they are formed into many shapes, from flat to curved. While quite durable (their expected life span is 25 to 40 years), concrete tiles are heavy and require proper roof-framing support.

Like clay tiles, concrete tiles may occasionally require treatment against discoloration. Often, when roofers recommend that they be replaced, the tiles can simply be repaired.

As a rough rule, if 25 percent or more of the asphalt shingles, wood shakes or shingles, or slate on a roof is in bad shape, the entire roof will have to be replaced.

With a flat roof, more typical of inexpensive housing or commercial buildings, check that puddles don't develop after a rain and that the covering doesn't have bubbles or tears.

Visit the attic and inspect the underside of any roof. Are there discolored areas from leaks? If the roof is shingles or shakes, can you see daylight? (Rain will expand the wood, sealing off leaks.) (See Figure 12-4.)

Ask the homeowner how old the roof is. That's your best clue to how much longer the roof may last. Asphalt shingles may last 20 to 25 years; wood shingles, 25 years; shakes, 40 years; slate tiles, 30 to 40 years; terra cotta tiles, 50 to 100 years; and roll roofing paper, the cheapest, 10 years.

Bear in mind that one-story houses have larger roofs than two- or three-story houses, so replacing the roof in a one-story house is typically far more expensive. Also keep in mind that a roof with a steep pitch is less likely to leak (water will flow off faster), but is also more dangerous for the homeowner to climb onto.

Figure 12-4.   Discolored areas under roof show leakage.

GUTTERS AND LEADERS

Gutters, which capture rainwater, may be made of wood, which, unfortunately, deteriorates and eventually must be replaced. Older gutters may also have been made of copper, and if the color has turned green, it's probably time for a replacement. The best choices are aluminum or plastic. (See Figure 12-5.)

See that the gutters have a good pitch and that they are protected from leaves and twigs by a gutter guard. Otherwise, they will clog and water may back up and destroy the wood behind them. (See Figure 12-6.)

The leaders or downspouts should also be clear: You can test the system by visiting a house when it's raining or—when it's not raining—by directing a hose of water onto the roof.

The leaders should discharge rainwater away from the house— ideally, to a drain where it flows to the street or to a drywell. If the water is discharged to the soil, it should be at a pitch or onto splash blocks, so that the water flows away from the house and not toward the foundation. (It will help if the dirt is graded away from the house.) If the rainwater just discharges into the soil, check the basement near that area for leaks. (See Chapter 27.)

Figure 12-5. **Gutters and leaders (downspouts).**

Figure 12-6.   Gutters clogged up with leaves.

Questions to ask the homeowner: How old is the roofing material? What kind is it? Have you had any leaks? Do you regularly have the gutters and leaders cleaned out? Has your basement ever leaked?

Hanging gutters are the most common. Built-in (New England) gutters are the kind that are integral with the roof. Such gutters are usually made of wood, often with metal or bituminous linings. They are difficult to inspect and to maintain. But if they are not maintained, they can lead to serious water penetration problems and to wood decay. A professional roofer should check and maintain built-in gutters, clearing them periodically of silt and rot-producing leaves. Ask the homeowner if he or she used a roofer on a regular basis.

MAINTAINING A ROOF

- Keep trees trimmed to prevent scuffing of the roof shingles by branches, or damage from falling limbs.

- Be careful not to puncture the roof covering when you install guy wires and television antennas.

- Promptly replace missing or damaged shingles.
- Don't walk directly on the roof. It's dangerous and can damage shingles. Use walk boards, ladders, or other protective devices.
- Check valley areas every year. Look for torn, worn, or lifted spots.
- Check the underside of the roof for signs of leakage, especially around vent pipes and chimneys.
- Watch for any signs of mold or sheathing delamination.
- Maintain good ventilation in the attic, even during winter months. An automatic vent fan is a good idea. Poor attic ventilation can cause severe damage to a roof.
- In sections of the country with heavy snowfall and subfreezing temperatures, be on the alert for ice dams, which form over the gutters on the eaves. They may cause water damage to the interior ceilings and walls.

If you need a new roof, consider laying the new shingles over the old ones. Most roof framing is designed to withstand the weight of two layers of shingles. The old roofing will provide additional insulation, and you can lay the new shingles without exposing the roof sheathing to the elements. You also bypass the labor expense and the mess of having the old covering removed, which could amount to half the cost of a new roof.

Red Flags

- ✔ Signs of patching on the roof; the entire roof sags.
- ✔ Asphalt shingles are curled, broken, or cracked; their color varies; they have few granules left on them.
- ✔ Two layers of shingles can be seen.
- ✔ Wood shingles or shakes are cracked, thin, or worn away.
- ✔ Slates are missing; some are cracked or flaked; nails are rusty.
- ✔ Broken or missing clay tiles.
- ✔ Some 25 percent of the roof materials needs replacement.
- ✔ You can see daylight from the underside of an attic, or water stains.
- ✔ The gutters, made of copper, have turned green.
- ✔ Built-in wood gutters.
- ✔ Areas of a supposedly entirely new roof aren't visible. (The owner may have replaced only the visible part of the roof.)

13

GARAGES

An attached garage has advantages over a detached garage. It lets you bring shopping bags directly into the house, and, come winter, the car or cars in your garage will get some heat from the house. It's usually good for a garage to be near the kitchen.

Detached garages will probably be old and in sorry shape. Many have been totally neglected by the homeowners but not by termites and other such insects (and rodents). But they may offer more storage space and some shelter for a car or two.

A two-car garage is far superior to a one-car garage; even one-car families can make use of the extra storage space. If there's no garage at all, check whether there's space and if the zoning codes would permit one. (Many houses just have carports.)

Inspect the walls and (in detached garages) the roof just as you would the house itself. Are they straight? Are they sagging? Do the shingles need replacing? A garage should also have plenty of shelving or room for shelving. The less clutter on the floor, the better.

Replacing a garage door can be expensive. If it's wood and it touches the ground, use a screwdriver to check the bottom for softness. A motorized garage door is a plus, especially the type where the door stops in its tracks if it encounters resistance—like a child's toy. (See Figure 13-1.) If the door isn't motorized, make sure the younger members of your family can lift it. The door should close tightly, to keep out rain, cold, heat, and animals. It should have a lock. Swing-up doors aren't as sturdy as fold-up doors.

In an attached garage, the wall next to the house and the ceiling should be fire-resistant—made of plaster, wallboard, or such. The door leading to the house should also be fire-resistant; it might even

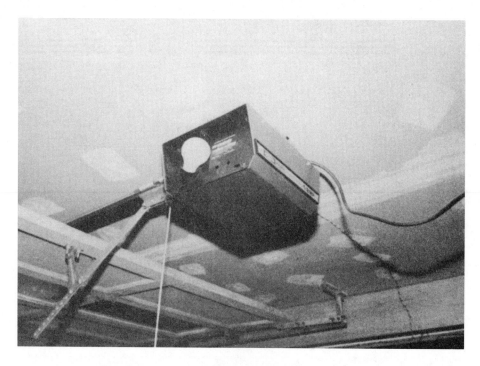

Figure 13-1.   Automatic garage-door opener.

be made of metal. It should be weatherstripped, too, to prevent fumes from the garage (from a car, from paint) from seeping into the house. If the floor of the room next to the garage's interior door is level with the garage floor, there should be a raised platform at the doorway to trap heavy gases inside the garage.

If the floor is concrete, check it for cracks. And check the levelness of the floor: you certainly don't want it pitched toward the house. Look for signs of water penetration, particularly if the driveway slopes toward the garage. Don't assume that termites aren't interested in the garage framing.

A garage should have adequate lighting, at least one electrical outlet (for appliances like a car vacuum cleaner), a window, and a faucet (on the wall next to the house—so the pipes are less likely to freeze).

Red Flags

✔ No garage and no space for one.

✔ The door is wood and soft at the bottom.

✔ The garage door is motorized, but doesn't stop readily if it encounters resistance.

✔ The floor is cracked.
✔ There are no electrical outlets, no lighting, no faucet.
✔ The walls are banged up.
✔ Your cars won't fit the space.

14

SWIMMING POOLS

Pools can be a source of healthy exercise and friendly socializing, a place where a family can relax. In well-to-do, warm weather areas, they may even add to the value of a house. On the other hand, they can be a royal pain in the neck—like luxurious yachts that spend much of their time in dry dock undergoing repairs.

POOL OPERATION

From the homeowner or builder, obtain the operating directions: Every pool system will have its own special features and requirements.

- Maintenance—Make sure that the owners have maintained the pool properly. Ask them which local pool maintenance firms they have used, and ask for receipts.
- Heaters—Is there a solar cover? Are the filtration system and the heating timer coordinated, so that the filter is running whenever the pool is being heated?
- Lighting and electrical—All pool lights should be grounded, of course. Area lighting itself should be of the low-voltage type, to minimize the risk of shock. Look for ground fault circuit interruptors. (See Figure 14-1.)
- Diving boards—A pool without one may be the best idea. If there was a board and it was replaced, make sure that the new one properly matches the pool's dimensions.
- Automatic pool cleaners—Very desirable. These units will

Figure 14-1.   Pool electric panel with ground fault
interruptors.

eliminate the boredom of pool vacuuming, and they can be
used with most pools, whatever their shape.

• Whether or not the community requires proper fencing and
gate locks, make sure that yours has them.

TYPES OF POOLS

In-ground swimming pools are either made of concrete or are lined
with vinyl or fiberglass. Concrete pools use rebars (steel rods) in the
walls and floor for extra stability. Concrete may be cast in place or
sprayed onto the metal framing of a pool (Gunite).

The inside surfaces of pools are usually plastered or painted, in
colors ranging from white to black. Tile may be used along the water
line, for easier maintenance and for appearance.

Only pools built in a straight line can be made of masonry
blocks. Reinforcement rods are inserted into the cores, which are
then filled with mortar. The final product is then either plastered
or painted.

Vinyl-lined pools are installed over metal, plastic, masonry block,
or wood framing, with a soft base (sand, fibrous material, etc.) or a
rigid base (concrete). Most such pools are rectangular, though other

shapes are possible. The liners themselves come in a variety of colors and designs.

Fiberglass pools are either a solid shell or a sectioned design. They don't need much maintenance, and they last a long time. Also, they come in a variety of built-in colors. In areas of high water alkalinity, improperly treated pool water can chalk the finish, necessitating a painting.

POOL FILTRATION

A pool, most of all, needs a properly working filtration system. Such a system enables homeowners to save water by using the initial water over and over again.

Most filtration systems consist of a filter (tank), pump, motor, supply and return piping, along with the pool elements, such as surface skimmers and drains. (Skimmers are receptacles at water level to draw off surface debris, oil, leaves, and so forth.)

There are three basic types of pool filters:

- High-rate sand;
- Pressure diatomaceous earth (D.E.); and
- Cartridge.

Check with your local water authorities for their recommendations about filters and their requirements.

1. High-rate sand filters—These dome-shaped filters are pressurized to provide a steady flow of water through the filtering sand. As the pool water is forced through the special sand bed, dirt particles are trapped.

2. Pressure D.E. filters—These more compact filters are more effective than sand filters, and require less water to backwash (remove the dirt particles). They use diatomaceous earth as the filter medium. This substance is a sedimentary rock composed of microscopic fossil skeletons of the diatom, a small water animal. The skeletons have a highly porous structure of silica, which makes them unaffected by most chemicals. The D.E. coats the filter's cloth-like membranes or tubes, which trap the sediment and dirt. (Check with local authorities on backwash restrictions because the D.E. filters can clog drywells used for backwashing.) (See Figure 14-2.)

3. Cartridge filters—This type of filter is gaining in popularity because it's less expensive both to buy and to operate. The

Figure 14-2.   Pool D.E. filters and water heater.

system's filter cartridges, which must be replaced periodically, are low in cost. On the other hand, this filter isn't able to consistently filter out the smaller dirt particles.

All three filter systems require backwashing. A pressure gauge will signal the need for backwashing when the pressure changes.

PRECLOSING INSPECTION

Before you actually buy the house, have the current owners review the entire pool operation, stressing the filtration system, the pool cleaner, and the pool heater. Survey the entire pool area for any signs of malfunction, from cracks in the pool floor on down the line.

Obtain all pool and equipment manuals and warranties. Get the name and address of the original pool-installation company and the current service company.

Red Flags

✔ The owners didn't seem to use the pool or have it serviced regularly.

✔ There are cracks in the pool floor, the filter doesn't seem to work, and so forth.

✔ No protective fencing around pool.

✔ No water in the pool.

✔ Algae in the pool water.

V

INSIDE THE HOUSE

15

INTERIOR DESIGN

For efficient traffic in a house, while you're in Room A, ideally you shouldn't have to enter Room B to get into Room C.

Another rule: Similar things should also be near one another, dissimilar things should be apart.

There are three general areas in a house, and they should be near one another: the work area (kitchen and laundry), the living area (living room, dining room, den), and the sleeping area (the bedrooms).

The kitchen is likely to be warm, what with the range and oven, so it should be on the cool (east or north) side of the house. It should overlook the yard, so parents can cook and watch the kids at the same time. It should also be next to the den, in case the kids are playing there, as well as the dining area. Also, it should be close to the garage, so you can easily bring in groceries from the car.

The laundry area might be next to the kitchen, or in the basement, or off the bedroom. It should have plenty of storage space, and plenty of countertop area for sorting and folding clothes.

Other desirable features of a house:

- The front door should open into a foyer, not into the living room. That will keep the remainder of the house protected from icy blasts in winter. Also, with a foyer, visitors can take off their wet things without dripping all over the living room.

- The stairway to a second floor or attic or to the basement shouldn't take up valuable floor space. Stairways should be located off hallways and foyers.

- The garage should accommodate at least two cars, because you'll probably want extra storage space there.

- Visitors shouldn't be able to peer into bedrooms. That way, when you straighten up for guests, you can ignore the bedrooms. Nor should visitors be able to peer into your kitchen, a "messy, informal area," as one architect calls it. In general, formal and informal areas, private and public areas, should be separate.

- The master bedroom should be in the back of the house, for quiet. An exception is if another side has a splendid view.

- A bathroom for guests should be in a private area, not by the entrance or kitchen. Windows in most bathrooms could be larger, for better ventilation.

- Rooms should be conventionally shaped or you may have trouble fitting in furniture. Avoid severely L-shaped rooms, for example.

- Fireplaces should be to the side of a room, so people walking through don't disturb those enjoying the fire.

- Large windows should display the best views—not necessarily in front of a house, where you may just see a street and other houses. All windows should be designed to make them energy-efficient, so they contain heat in winter, cool air in summer.

MEMORABLE MISTAKES

Mistakes in interior design can mean wasted steps and lost time, impatience and annoyance—even danger. Here are some design mistakes that architects have witnessed:

- Bedrooms in a below-grade basement—when the windows are too high and too small to allow occupants to leave quickly in an emergency, like a fire. In one case, access to a house's basement apartment was through a garage stairway—and garages, with gas-powered cars, gas-powered lawnmowers, and flammable paints, are dangerous rooms.

- A kitchen where the range was between the refrigerator and the sink. It's better for the sink to be in between—so you can take food from the fridge, get water from the sink, then move over to the range. (See Figure 15-1.)

- A bungalow with two bedrooms in the attic, and the only way to get into the attic was through a stairway through the bathroom. What if the bathroom was occupied when someone wanted to enter or leave a bedroom?

- A new bedroom constructed in the back of a house so you have to go through the kitchen and bedroom to reach the backyard.

Figure 15-1.   Convenient kitchen layout.

- A house where the only way to walk into the kitchen, from the garage, was through the dining room, so you had to carry groceries through a formal room to put them away.

Red Flags

✔ You must go into room B to get from room A to room C. (Exception: A little-used room, like an office off a living room, can be a "dead-end.")

✔ The three chief areas of a house aren't compact: the work area (kitchen and laundry), the living area (living room, dining room, den), and the sleeping area (the bedrooms).

✔ The kitchen doesn't overlook the yard and isn't next to the playroom; the garage isn't next to the kitchen.

✔ There's no foyer when visitors enter.

✔ Visitors can peer into bedrooms or into the kitchen.

✔ Small windows everywhere.

✔ Not enough closet space.

✔ High noise transmission throughout house.

16

FIREPLACES
AND CHIMNEYS

A young couple bought a house with a lovely fireplace not long ago, and celebrated their maiden night as first-time homeowners by lighting a cheerful, crackling fire. They then discovered that it was a non-working fireplace.

Fireplaces—artificial as well as real—do sell houses. Few if any additions add more value to a house, dollar for dollar, than a fireplace. Some homeowners like roaring fires in the fireplace so much that, in the middle of summer, they turn on all the air conditioners—and start a fire.

Your first concern with a fireplace is: Is it safe? Is there evidence that it has been used, like ashes in the firebox and darkened firebrick? If not, perhaps the homeowners gave up on it because it was smoky. Or, at a minimum, the homeowners didn't know how to build a fire properly.

If there's soot and smudges on the front of the fireplace, that's reassuring—it's a working fireplace. But it can also be worrisome that the fire or smoke spread beyond the firebox.

Three immediate steps you should take:

- Check that the chimney is the highest part of the house. It should extend at least two feet above any ridge within a ten-foot diameter, and three feet above flat roofs. Otherwise sparks from a chimney could be a problem, and you could get downdrafts—wind blowing down the chimney and into your house.

- Using a flashlight, peer up the chimney. Is there a fireproof material lining the inside of the chimney, like tile or clay, or are there just bricks or stones and mortar? Installing a fireproof flue can be expensive. (See Figure 16-1.) Also, are there any signs of a creosote buildup in the chimney? (Creosote is a black, gummy, highly combustible substance that forms on chimney and stove-pipe interiors.) If there is, call a chimney sweep before using the fireplace.

- With the homeowner's or real estate agent's permission, burn a newspaper in the fireplace, to check that the smoke rises readily up the chimney flue—and don't forget to open the damper. (Open windows or doors in the house first, to provide air to replace the air that rises up the chimney.)

If you have any doubts about the safety of a fireplace, ask someone from the local fire department to make an inspection.

Check that the fireplace has a damper, a metal cover that closes off the opening in the flue, and that it works smoothly. Some fireplaces in older houses don't have dampers, and they aren't an absolute necessity (if you don't care about heat loss). The best dampers are adjustable, by means of a handle, so you can keep the flue open enough to draw smoke but not so open as to draw heat away from the house.

Inspect the chimney bricks and mortar, inside and outside, to make sure they don't need repair. (See Figure 16-2.)

The chimney should be capped with a cover, to keep water out, and the opening covered with wire, to protect against animals. (See

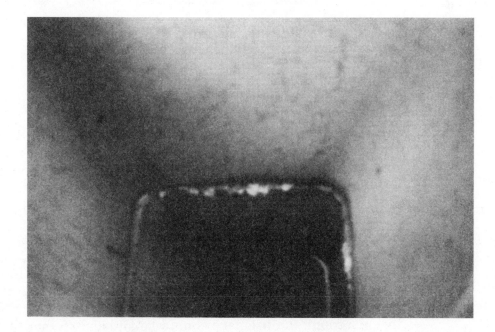

Figure 16-1.   Flue pipe inside chimney.

Figure 16-2.   Chimney pulling away from house.

Figure 16-3.) Don't laugh. Trying to escort a squirrel in your fireplace out of the house is no picnic.

See whether there's a working ash pit in the rear or floor of the firebox, where ashes can be brushed down a chute to the basement or to an ash cleanout on the outside of the house, for removal later. There should be a metal door at the removal end, to prevent hot ashes from falling on combustible materials. (See Figure 16-4.)

Make sure that there's a screen in front of the fireplace and a nonflammable hearth in front. (See Figure 16-5.) The hearth should extend 24 inches into a room and 8 inches on both sides of the fireplace opening, as protection against sparks and burning embers.

A fireplace ideally should be away from the outside walls, so any heat will eventually go into the house rather than outside. Inside a room, the fireplace should be situated so that the largest number of people can gather in front. The fireplace itself should

Figure 16-3.   Chimney shield.

match the size of the room: It shouldn't be so grandiose that it overwhelms a room.

If the fireplace has a mantel, check that it's level. Also make sure that the fireplace and chimney, usually the heaviest part of a house, aren't settling unevenly into the ground.

Ask the owners: Do they use the fireplace? How often? Is it smoky? What advice can they give you about building a fire? (If they really use it, they should be eager to provide advice, such as that building the fire atop bricks, in the rear of the firebox, can help prevent smokiness, as can burning paper in the firebox first to preheat the flue and improve smoke flow upward.)

Also ask the owners whether the andirons and other fireplace equipment go with the house.

A newer type of fireplace screen has glass doors to seal off the firebox, so that you can go to sleep with a fire winding down and not worry about the house burning down.

Figure 16-4.   Fireplace cleanout.

Figure 16-5.   Fireplace with nonflammable hearth.

GOOD FIREPLACE HABITS

As a source of heat, fireplaces have two drawbacks:

- By drawing heated air from a room and up the chimney, they make your heating system work harder; and
- The heat that a fireplace provides is mainly direct radiation. Only objects directly in line with the fireplace will feel warm. On the other hand, a heating system heats the air, which heats you, so you will feel warm regardless of where you are in relationship to the source.

Here are some suggestions so that your energy dollars don't go up in smoke:

- The wood supply left by the former homeowner should be dry. It takes energy to dry up any moisture. Also, the firewood pile should be away from the house, so you don't help insects enter your home.
- If the fireplace is never used, seal the damper with fibrous glass insulation stuffed in the chimney, and use a gasket around the damper, to prevent heat loss or the loss of cooled air.
- A heat circulator may be a plus. Some types are simply hollow grates that sit in the fireplace; others use fans to circulate more heated air.
- A glass door allows radiant heat into a room, while decreasing the amount of air drawn up the chimney.

WOOD-BURNING STOVES

In recent years, partially in response to high utility bills, many homeowners have installed wood-burning stoves and fireplace inserts. It's vital that manufacturers' installation and operating instructions be followed and that the stove complies with local municipal requirements (including the necessary permits). (See Figure 16-6.)

Since both stoves and inserts burn wood at lower operating temperatures than conventional fireplaces, they accumulate creosote at a fairly fast rate. Most fireplace/stove/insert fires are caused by creosote ignition; the fire is very intense. That's why you should regularly check for creosote buildup.

Figure 16-6.   Wood-burning fireplace insert.

Red Flags

✔ The fireplace doesn't seem to have been used; perhaps the owners found it too smoky.

✔ The chimney is not the highest part of the house.

✔ The chimney is lined with just mortar and bricks or stones.

✔ You see creosote in the chimney.

✔ You see cracks in the firebricks or mortar.

✔ A wood-burning stove wasn't installed according to the manufacturer's specifications.

✔ There are smoke stains outside the fire box.

17

FLOORS

As important as having a good roof over your head is having sound floors below your feet. As you walk through a house, begin your evaluation of the flooring.

Walk heavily (not quite a jump) as you check out each room. The floors should feel solid as you tread on them, with no bounciness, squeakiness, or crunchiness. Bounciness means that there could be separation between the flooring and the sub-flooring/floor joists. Squeakiness indicates possible shrinkage of the flooring, loose or missing bridging, or warpage. Crunchiness under floor coverings may indicate moisture damage to the sub-flooring.

While your feet are doing the walking, pay attention to the levelness of the floors and stairways. (A marble will roll across an uneven floor without being pushed.) Also pay attention to the type of floors and floor coverings throughout the house.

Every house will settle some over time. But floors and stairs should not be far out of plumb. Excess settlement indicates a structural deficiency.

You will also notice that doors in houses with excessive settlement won't close easily and snugly unless the door bottoms have been cut to accommodate the settling. Watch for replaced or repositioned baseboards, intended to cover up telltale gaps at the wall/floor junctions.

Floors can be covered with wood flooring, resilient flooring, or carpeting/tile over sub-flooring. Wood flooring can be made of hardwoods such as oak, maple, birch, beech, and pecan, or the less expensive softwoods like pine, elm, hemlock, and larch. Wood flooring comes in various types, such as boards, planks, and parquet (small sections of wood pressed together to form tiles).

Resilient flooring takes the form of linoleum, vinyl, rubber, asphalt, and so forth, in sheet and tile products. It's glued to a sub-flooring, which must be substantial enough to provide rigidity to the floor.

Tiles made of marble, adobe, slate, or ceramic materials are often found in foyers, kitchens, and bathrooms. Broader use of these durable floor coverings is found in more expensive houses.

If the floors are covered with wall-to-wall carpeting, lift up a corner (with the homeowner's permission) to determine the type of flooring under the carpeting and its condition, if possible. Also, note any stains on the carpeting. It could be in an area where household plants were kept and watered. Or the stain could indicate a pet's favorite spot. In any case, the area below these stain spots could have moisture damage or severe staining of the wood flooring.

Carpeting can be lush, restful, warm, quieting, and fairly inexpensive to install and replace at a later date. The best carpeting is stain-resistant and high density (more fibers per inch).

Red Flags

✔ A floor doesn't feel solid as you walk on it, and you feel bounciness, squeakiness, or crunchiness.

✔ The floor isn't level. If you're in doubt, see if a marble rolls across the floor without being pushed.

✔ Doors don't close easily; there may have been a lot of settlement. Check whether the door bottoms have been cut to accommodate the settling. Be alert for replaced or repositioned baseboards, intended to cover up telltale gaps at the places where walls and floors meet.

✔ A stain on a carpet may indicate an area where the wood underneath has been damaged.

✔ You see portable screw-jack support columns in basement (they could indicate a structural deficiency).

18

WALLS AND CEILINGS

The last thing you want to see on walls or ceilings is water stains. One reason is that it can be murder to determine where they came from, which means it may be quite a while before you establish their origin. Water leaking from the attic or from a bathroom can take bizarre circuitous routes before it exits somewhere.

You do want walls and ceilings that are straight and durable, without bumps, cracks, peeling paint, nail pops, bubbles in wall-paper, or other imperfections. Recent obvious repairs are also a reason to worry. They mean you must examine every wall in the house.

If you're seriously interested in a house, don't just check three walls in a room and neglect the one that's covered with paintings or photographs. Look behind the paintings and photographs—and the furniture, too. If everything in a room is painted but the area behind a bookcase, and the owners take that bookcase with them, the entire room may have to be repainted. Worse yet, the bookcase may be concealing a bulge in the wall or a crack. Your preclosing inspection will give you one final chance to look at the house, when it's uncluttered with furniture, rugs, frames, and so forth.

Walls are commonly made of plaster, paneling (ideally over sheetrock), or masonry (brick or stone).

Walls and ceilings may be covered the old-fashioned way, with plaster applied wet to wiring and lathing, or with gypsum board (also called dryboard or sheetrock). Plaster is hard and durable, good for soundproofing, and relatively expensive; it's also is likely to develop harmless cracks. Gypsum board is less expensive, cheaper to install, and easier to repair. But if an amateur put it up, you can usually tell: The seams between the boards will be noticeable, and eventually nails or screws may start popping out.

Paneling—usually made of solid wood, plywood, or pressed board—is also durable, but its attractiveness depends on its quality and how professionally it was installed. If an amateur did the job, you may be able to see the nail holes, and even spot gaps between the panels. To check that the panels were installed over properly spaced framing (a stud every 16 inches is preferred) and sheetrock, carefully press on them in various locations. You shouldn't feel much give.

Check the trim for signs of water stains. Any discoloration or warping may indicate a water penetration problem behind the paneling.

Do the walls and ceilings do a good job of soundproofing? Have someone talk upstairs or in the next room and listen intently.

Wallpaper is usually fancier than paint, but more expensive to apply—especially if you must remove old layers first. A house inhabited by young children who have access to crayons may be better off with painted walls rather than wallpaper.

Finally, electrical outlets should be at six-foot intervals for convenience. Most homeowners prefer a wall switch to control room lighting.

Red Flags

✔ Water stains on the ceilings or walls.

✔ Walls or ceilings with bumps, cracks, peeling paint, nail pops, or bubbles in wallpaper.

✔ Recent repairs.

✔ Paneling that was installed by the seller rather than by a professional.

✔ Paneling that has a lot of give—meaning that it may not have been installed properly.

✔ Wallpaper that must be removed and that consists of several layers or has been painted over.

✔ The baseboard molding has been replaced (perhaps to conceal the unevenness caused by the house's settling).

✔ Too few wall outlets; no lighting-wall switch.

19

DOORS AND WINDOWS

INSIDE AND OUTSIDE DOORS

Smart sellers know that a front door is vital in giving would-be buyers a good first impression. If the front door of a house is in bad shape, don't get your hopes up.

One of the basic things you should check with an outside door is: How tight is the fit? Look up and down the edges. Can you see light? Examine the bottom. How is cold air prevented from coming in during winter, and cool air from escaping in the summer? Is the threshhold in good condition? Is there weatherproofing? If the weather outside is breezy, put your hand over the door edges. Can you feel air coming in? Is there a storm door, with both glass and screen panels?

Outside doors may be flush (flat) or stile-and-rail (with panels). Make sure that the panels in stile-and-rail doors don't have small cracks. A kickplate over the bottom of the door will help keep the door in good condition.

Check all exterior doors. Don't overlook double-glazed (insulated) patio doors. Look for signs of a broken seal (condensation or moisture marks between the glass panels). The only remedy for a broken seal is full replacement of the door itself.

If the doors are sliding doors, check that they (as well as the screens) move back and forth easily, without popping out of their tracks. House settlement can warp the tracks and create a problem.

Also make sure that both inside and outside doors swing open and close easily, and that doors that you want to lock can lock (bathrooms, for instance).

Interior doors don't face the challenges of exterior doors and are generally in better shape. Still, open and shut them and check their condition. Solid wood doors have a long life unless house settlement has skewed them or their frames. The lower-priced hollow-core doors (a sandwich of wood veneers with pressed board fillers), on the other hand, will dry out and require replacement.

As you check any hollow-core doors, listen for any interior-filler movement. Make sure that there are keys for any doors with locks, or learn how to open a locked door from the outside. Parents of young children, take heed: Keep a door-opening device near doors that can be locked.

Houses with forced-air heating or central air conditioning—and no individual room returns—should have interior doors with gaps at the bottom to allow room air to reach the central air returns when the doors are closed.

For advice about security for doors and windows, see Chapter 29.

WINDOWS

Casement windows are those you crank open and shut, and many homeowners and home inspectors absolutely loathe them. The metal variety tend to rust, and the cranking mechanism can gum up. Finding replacement parts for older casement window mechanisms can be a hassle. Also, you will need special air conditioners for such windows. (See Figure 19-1.)

Double-hung windows are those that come in two sections, which slide up and down. Modern versions are made of wood with vinyl covering (vinyl-clad) and can be tilted for cleaning. The older, wooden versions sometimes stick and won't remain open or shut— the top one is forever falling down. Replacing a defective pulley mechanism in a window can be expensive; channel springs can be installed at a fraction of the cost.

Newer windows are double-glazed or even triple-glazed—in effect, the units are twice or three times as thick as conventional windows, with air between the layers acting as insulation. If the glass is cloudy, water has gotten between the layers. If the windows aren't at least double-glazed, they should have storm windows to conserve energy.

As with outside doors, make sure that no cold air is coming through the sides of windows and that you cannot see light at the edges. The windows themselves should be tight in their frames, and if putty is holding the glass, the putty should not be dry and fragile. Such putty should be replaced.

Open and shut all windows to make sure they're working. Wood windows are better than metal, partly because wood is a better insulator.

Figure 19-1.   Vertical casement window.

Make sure that the rooms have enough windows to provide adequate light. Window openings should make up about 10 percent of the wall surfaces in a room. If it's daytime and the window drapes are pulled back, all the room's lights are on, and the room is full of mirrors, be worried.

If there are skylights, check them for leakage. Are there stains next to the skylights on the ceilings? Can you see where fresh tar has been applied around the exterior of the skylights? Skylights are notorious for leaking, so be careful. (See Figure 19-2.)

Red Flags

✔ You see light through the edges of exterior doors.

✔ You feel a draft through the sides of exterior doors or at the bottom.

✔ The sliding-door easily pops out of its track.

Figure 19-2.   Skylights.

✔ Casement windows aren't working smoothly or closing completely.

✔ A double-hung window doesn't want to remain shut or open.

✔ Hollow-core interior doors rattle when opened and closed rapidly.

✔ There aren't enough windows in a room or enough window area to provide adequate light.

✔ There are signs of leakage around skylights.

20

KITCHENS

The kitchen may be the single most important room in a house, for three reasons:

1. When people choose a house to buy, the kitchen tends to be decisive;

2. The kitchen is where much of a family's time is spent; and

3. Repairs and renovations of kitchens tend to be the most expensive home improvement.

To begin with, ask yourself: Is the kitchen modern? Is there plenty of lighting—track lighting for the work areas, for instance? What is the layout, capacity, and condition of the cabinets? Are there new appliances, along with a microwave oven, convection oven, and garbage disposal? (See Figure 20-1.)

Is the regular oven self-cleaning? Is there a double oven? Is it the kind where a built-in sparker lights the gas? Is there a built-in dishwasher right next to the sink? Is the sink stainless steel? Are there two sinks, one for washing and one for draining dishes? Is there plenty of closet space?

Is there room for a dining nook, so that breakfasts and snacking don't have to be carried on in the dining room? Is the kitchen itself bright and sunny, from windows or skylights? Is there a pantry? A broom closet?

Make sure that the sink area, the oven, and the refrigerator—the kitchen triangle—are close together. The total of the sides of the triangle should be not less than 12 feet and no more than 22 feet. Each side should be between 4 feet and 9 feet. In other words, the

Figure 20-1.   Microwave oven over electric range.

distance between either of the appliances and the sink should be between 4 and 9 feet.

There should be an exhaust fan above the stove, along with a grease guard. (See Figure 20-2.) The wall next to the stove and the surface behind the stove should be fireproof.

Countertop materials may be wood, ceramic tile, Corian, stainless steel, or plastic laminate. The counter area should be at least 2 feet wide, 20 feet long, and ideally stretching out on both sides of the sink. If there's anything on the counter (a cutting board, a hot tray), peek underneath, to make sure that they aren't concealing permanent stains or burns.

Check the splashboard—where the countertop meets the wall behind the sink area. Unless it's molded as part of the countertop or is well sealed, you will experience water spillage behind the countertop cabinets.

Also make sure there is a toehold at the bottom of all work area cabinets; without a place for your toes to go, you will work leaning over, and may develop a sore back. None of the doors of the appliances, if open, should block the path of anyone walking through the kitchen.

On your preclosing walk-through inspection, turn on all the appliances. If the refrigerator has been turned off and the door left

Figure 20-2.   Exhaust fan over range.

closed, you can expect odors. Place a bowl or two of charcoal briquettes in the refrigerator to absorb the odor; follow up with an open box of baking powder. Check the seals around the door; look for signs of water spillage below the unit. The refrigerator should run quietly.

The dishwasher should also run quietly, and not leak a drop. To make sure that water is washing everything, leave a cup or saucer in the top part, to make sure it collects water. (This shows that the upper spray is working.) Look for signs of leakage in the floor around the dishwasher.

A clothes washer should run quietly and not "walk" while it's on. Check for rust where the rubber hoses connect in the back. A drier should be properly vented to the outside, so that moisture can escape, and also work quietly and efficiently. If you will be installing an electric dryer, be sure there is 220-volt power to the house and a 220-volt outlet to plug the dryer into.

Ask about the age of the appliances and whether there are still warranties. Obtain copies.

Count the number of electrical outlets. There should be one for every three feet of counter space. They should be grounded, preferably with ground fault circuit interrupters (GFCI) for those outlets near the sink area. In these modern times, the kitchen should also have a phone.

Check the water pressure in the sink—first the cold and then the hot. Are there turn-off valves under the sink, in case repairs are needed? Do they work? Are there any signs of water leakage or stains? Make sure there is a U-shaped trap under the sink, to trap sewage gas. If there's a rinse spray gun, see if it works. Most of the spray guns stop working after a spell.

Fill the sink halfway full of water and let it drain. Does it drain quickly? Do you hear a gurgling sound? That's a worrisome sign that the trap isn't full of water, as it should be.

Also, have you had the water tested? Even municipal water systems may not be living up to the federal water standards, particularly with regard to lead. Well system water should be tested, at a minimum, for bacteria levels. Check with your municipal offices and ask about any local water problems. (See Chapter 6.)

Finally—and we're sorry we have to mention it—look for signs of ants, cockroaches, and other nasty creatures. Many of these critters have a sweet tooth—hence, the appeal of the kitchen. Traps hidden behind appliances are a tip-off. Remember, roaches are nocturnal; visit the house after dark, go right to the kitchen, and flip on the lights. Let's hope that you—and they—won't be surprised.

Red Flags

✔ The kitchen is dark and old-fashioned, with old appliances and not much storage space.

✔ There's no room for a dining nook.

✔ The refrigerator, oven, and sink aren't close together.

✔ The appliances don't seem to be working properly, or they are very old.

✔ There aren't enough electrical outlets and no GFCIs.

✔ The water pressure in the sink isn't strong.

✔ There are insect traps hidden behind appliances.

✔ The countertops are old and worn.

✔ The cabinets are not adequately secured to the walls.

21

BATHROOMS

As far as house value goes, bathrooms are exceeded in importance only by kitchens. So, when you go shopping for a house, be sure to give the bathrooms a thorough going-over.

To begin with, there should be enough. At least one-and-a-half for every two bedrooms is the rule. Another guideline is to have one on every floor. A full bath contains a sink, toilet, and shower or tub. A half-bath has just a sink and toilet. A half-bath is probably satisfactory in a foyer or basement. The most luxurious full bath should be next to the master bedroom.

Even before inspecting bathrooms, check something else first: the ceilings of rooms directly underneath bathrooms. Look for stains or other signs of leakage.

Ideally, a bathroom will have a tile floor and half-tiled walls. The least desirable is wooden floors, which might be damaged by moisture. Lift up any bathroom carpeting; it might be concealing a water-damaged floor. Check around the toilets. Any water leakage from a defective seal may cause rotting.

The faucets should be brand names. Light handles (made of zinc or aluminum) are the bargain variety. Can you shut off each faucet without any resulting drips?

Sinks of vitreous china resist chipping and acid that you might use to unclog a pipe. Marbleized units are pretty and easy to clean, but scratches aren't easy to remove. In this respect, Corian (a brand name) sinks are better. Their color goes all the way through the material. The least expensive and least desirable sinks are porcelain or enamel over cast iron or steel. They chip and stain more easily.

The basin, ideally, should have a double bowl. It should be large enough so that you can wash your hair. Look for rust, chips, or discoloration. Run the water. Is the flow strong and even? Check the hot and cold water separately. Does the water drain quickly?

The bathtub may be fiberglass (light and easy to clean, but noisy when water hits it); enameled cast iron or steel (sturdy, but it stains and chips); or—the high-priced spread—ceramic tiles. A safety bar should be next to the tub.

Make sure that the corners of a shower stall or bathtub, and where they attach to the floor, are properly caulked or grouted. (See Figure 21-1.) Incidentally, you apply caulk where you require flexibility, such as around a bathtub; you grout where you require rigidity, such as around ceramic tiles and at vertical wall joints.

Most water leaks in bathrooms are not the result of defective shower pans or defective plumbing, but simply water's penetrating cracked caulking or grouting. Defective grouting around bathroom tiles will allow water seepage behind the tile and the decay of the very backer board that supports the tile. You're talking big bucks when you are dealing with any extensive tile work. (See Figure 21-2.)

Is the mechanical drain plug working, or is there just a rubber or plastic plug? Is there a waterproof shower light?

Check the shower and tub for drainage. Add water, and then flip the drain handle or turn the drain plug in the tub. The flow should be steady. Fill the tub to a level of six inches or so, and then open

Figure 21-1.   Poor shower caulking.

Figure 21-2.   Good grouting and caulking.

the drain to determine if the drainage is steady. Next, check the shower. If it's above the tub, check its operation—both hot and cold water. If the shower is a separate fixture, also check it also for drainage after running the water for several minutes.

These days, people want shower heads with multiple settings that can deliver anything from a torrent of water to needle-like jets. Check their operation during your shower test.

Glass or plastic sliding doors can be a problem to keep clean, so don't award them many points. Glass doors also raise a question of safety.

Toilets may be mounted on a wall, for design purposes and ease of cleaning, or on the floor. Be sure all toilets are secure; any wobbling may indicate a seal problem.

Test the toilet by flushing a small wad of rolled-up toilet tissue. Does the water back up quickly or does it flush smoothly? (Be ready to remove the tank cover and flip the plug over the drain line, to cut the water flow to the toilet. This is what you should do whenever you notice the water level rising in the toilet after a flush.) Also, does the bowl fill up in two minutes, or does it take seemingly forever? (That's a sign of an obstruction that needs clearing.) Is it quiet?

The best toilet bowls are the siphon-vortex or siphon-jet variety, which is quiet and does a good job of washing down the bowl during flushes. Its flushing action is accelerated by a stream of water forced into the trap at the back of the bowl, causing increased siphoning action.

A step below is the reverse-trap bowl. It features a trap in the back of the bowl.

The washdown bowl is what most of us have—somewhat noisier but economical. Water enters the toilet from the rear and from holes around the rim. As the water level rises over the lip of the trap at the front, a siphon action draws out the toilet contents.

The newer, water-conserving toilets use less water per flush but may not perform adequately for solid wastes (unless they're pressurized).

If the water in the bowl is blue from a germicide, ask whether the bottom of the bowl is stained or cracked. The germicide may have been introduced to conceal the damage.

If you can gain access to the toilet tank, check it for mildew and the metal parts for corrosion. Is the water clear? Is the flotation arm bent back? That's a sign that repairs may be needed.

A newer bathroom will have shut-off valves attached to every fixture, so you can make repairs without having to turn off all the water in the house. Test a few of the shut-off valves. Do they turn easily? After you turn them, does the water in the faucets above stop running? If this area is concealed, are there signs of leakage?

If you are serious about a house, check the water pressure. Run cold water in the sink, then cold water in the tub or shower, and then flush the toilet. Is there a noticeable drop in pressure? Now try it with hot water. Also, while you're checking the water pressure, check whether the water becomes hot quickly and stays hot.

Are there at least two electrical outlets in the bathroom? Are they grounded—will they accept three-prong appliances? Best of all would be ground fault circuit interruptors (GFCIs). No electrical outlet should be reachable from a bathtub or shower.

The lighting in a bathroom should be ample enough to permit you to enjoy that most civilized of habits—reading in the tub. If a bathroom has a window, be sure it's an insulated unit and that it's not in the area of a tub or shower; the moisture will eventually rot out the window framing.

Modern bathrooms should have electric exhaust systems controlled by a wall switch. Some have heaters built in. In your tour of the attic, make sure any exhausts are piped directly to the outside and not into the attic.

Is there a spacious medicine cabinet? While the bathroom isn't the ideal place to keep medications (moisture may not be good for them), that's where most people store them.

A linen closet is desirable. So is a bathroom large enough for the owners to add a whirlpool bath, steam bath, or sauna.

Are the walls covered by acrylic paint, waterproof wallpaper, or some other suitable material? If not, the bathroom may develop mildew, and the wall materials will deteriorate quickly.

In general, check a bathroom for leaks, cracks (in tile, porcelain), odors, stains, and mildew.

Red Flags

- ✔ There isn't one bathroom on every floor.
- ✔ Water doesn't drain from tub, basin, or shower quickly.
- ✔ There are water stains on the floor or walls, or on the ceiling of the room below.
- ✔ The floor is wood, which might be damaged by moisture.
- ✔ The caulking and grouting have worn away.
- ✔ The toilet bowl is noisy, the water rises ominously after you flush, and the bowl takes a long time to fill up.
- ✔ The water pressure seems low.
- ✔ There aren't enough electrical outlets, and existing ones aren't grounded.
- ✔ The floors crunch when you walk on them.

22

ATTICS

Some homeowners think that even unfinished attics should be airtight, to retain warmth inside the house. So, in the winter, they seal up their attics.

This is a serious mistake. Attics need ventilation, to discharge moisture. That's why they should have a vent window, a louvered vent, a turbine, or a powered vent fan. (See Figure 22-1.) Many homeowners make the mistake of covering up all their attic openings, including those small, round vents located in the soffits (the horizontal sheeting under the roof eaves).

Without ventilation, moisture may rot away the rafters and sheathing in an attic. Also, heat may build up in summer, straining the house's air-conditioning. So, one of the first things to check in an attic is that there's enough ventilation, even if it means that the place is frigid in winter.

If the attic isn't cold, snow on the roof will melt quickly. That's one reason people are warned against houses with roofs where the snow has melted before other snowy roofs have melted.

It's because an unfinished attic should be cold in winter that insulation should be in the ceiling floor, not underneath the roof. Be sure that the vapor barrier on any attic floor insulation is on the bottom facing the heated portion of the house. (This is true for all insulation.)

As for finished attics, they need ventilation, too—in the dead spaces behind walls and ceilings. There should be room for air circulation between the insulation and the roof.

Other things to check in attics:

- Be sure that the roof isn't bowed; it's a sure sign of a support problem. Pinpoint the precise cause of any bowing.

Figure 22-1.   Attic ventilation fan in roof.

Figure 22-2.   Unsafe open electrical-junction box in attic.

- Make sure that the pipes from bathrooms extend into the roof and don't end in the attic. If they do, moist, damaging air will be trapped in the attic.
- Check the underside of the roof for wet spots and for discolored areas where rain has penetrated. Use a screwdriver to poke the wood, to make sure it isn't so soft that it needs replacing.
- Any attic should have a light and an electrical outlet.
- Be alert for unfinished electrical work, such as improperly spliced lines and missing connection boxes. (See Figure 22-2.)
- Keep your eyes open for any signs of critter activity (droppings, gnawing, holes). Squirrels love to invade attics; they can be very destructive guests.

Red Flags

- ✔ The attic has no ventilation, and therefore may have excessive moisture.
- ✔ Snow on the roof melts quickly, before it has melted on the roofs of other houses.
- ✔ Insulation in an unfinished attic is in the ceiling, not in the floor.
- ✔ The roof is bowed.
- ✔ Exhaust pipes from the bathrooms end in the attic.
- ✔ Wet spots and discolored areas are visible on the underside of the roof, and the wood there is very soft.
- ✔ There's unfinished electrical work in the attic.
- ✔ There are signs that animals have been visiting.
- ✔ There's no ready access to the attic, which is a clue that no one has been checking it for problems.

23

BASEMENTS AND FOUNDATIONS

The conventional advice given to buyers is to go to the basement first. See the worst. The conventional advice given to sellers is not to let buyers see the basement last. It may leave them with a lingering negative memory of the house.

A well-known architect, William Ward, used to say sourly that the function of a basement is to collect water. But some basements are not just damp. They're also dark, dingy, and drafty.

Still, basements can house your home's heating, cooling, and plumbing systems as well as a workshop. They can provide basic storage. They could be finished for entertaining or as expanded playrooms.

BASEMENT PROBLEMS

As you go to the basement, check the lighting. Is it adequate? Even on the steps going down? The steps themselves should be safe, with a handrail in easy reach.

A telltale sign of basement water is that anything stored there is on raised platforms. Another telltale sign is a dehumidifier that's running or has been tucked away in a closet. Other signs of dampness include wet pipes, rusty nails in the floorboard, stained paneling, musty smell, rust anywhere, and smelly books. (See Figure 23-1.) Water stains on the floor are ambiguous: They might be from an overflowing washing machine.

Pay particular attention to the corners of the basement. The

Figure 23-1.   Water stains on basement paneling.

corners are where the downspouts are located on the outside; water is more likely to accumulate there and seep into the basement.

Look for signs of mildew and efflorescence (whitish, flaky mineral buildup). And don't be fooled by paneling on the walls; that's no guarantee that a basement is dry. A good sign is stacks of old magazines or books sitting on the basement floor, dry as a bone, collecting cobwebs.

Does the basement itself leak? The best way to find out is to be there after it has been raining for a while. Failing that, check for rust on any metal columns or other metal objects, such as a furnace or boiler. Is there a sump pump? You cannot always see a pump; ask the sellers. Check whether expensive furniture or clothing is kept down here.

Don't assume that a basement is dry just because there's no standing water during your house tour. It may not be the rainy or thawing season (spring).

Finally, get a statement from the present owners concerning the wetness of the basement. Many home inspectors will question the homeowners for you. Also, be just as cautious of houses without basements. Exterior conditions can also cause water problems in crawl spaces and first floor rooms.

If the basement or crawl space floor isn't dirt, count yourself fortunate. Many older houses do have dirt floors. Control of moisture is especially important with dirt floors. Keep dirt floor areas clear of debris, especially wood.

A cement floor is acceptable; tile or linoleum over cement would be better. Examine the floor for cracks.

Ideally, a basement has two exit doors: one into the house and one to the outside. (Most have only one exit, into the house.) It should also be roomy, in case you want to install an extra bedroom, sauna, or game room. Is the ceiling high enough so that you don't bump your head after you've installed lighting and a drop ceiling?

With a screwdriver, check any exposed wood for softness or decay, signs of termites, or dry rot. If a great deal of wood in various areas is decayed, it's time to get worried. Ask for evidence of any extermination companies' inspections, treatments, or guarantees. If the homeowners can't provide any, point out this situation to your home inspector if you decide to proceed with the purchase. (See Figure 23-2.)

Inspect the windows. Are there enough for fresh air and light? Do they open and close readily? Do they have screens as well as windows? Are they safe—with bars over them—or could a burglar just kick them in? Are there any signs of decay or insect infestation in the window framing?

Figure 23-2.   Termite damage to wood members.

A finished basement with a wet bar may seem attractive, but bear in mind that basements have lost much of their popularity: People no longer like living below the ground, if they ever did.

Time spent checking out the basement will pay dividends later should you wish to finish the basement for added bedroom space, storage, or recreation.

If the house doesn't have a basement, it was built on a concrete slab or over a crawl space. Check the slab for cracking; make sure there there's a vapor barrier (a layer of thick plastic) in the crawl space protecting the underside of the house from moisture.

SETTLEMENT PROBLEMS

Settlement is technically defined as the sinking of a building below its original position. Usually it's the result of an uneven foundation movement caused by the soil below it becoming more compacted. The compaction could be caused by anything from soil that had been previously disturbed (so it had not had time to settle down again) to soil whose moisture content suddenly changes (as soil dries, it becomes more compacted).

Sometimes the settlement is due to poor construction. The builder may have taken out too much soil and then replaced some—leaving a void, or uncompacted soil. Or the house may have been built on a landfill that wasn't properly compacted. In rare cases, settlement is caused by fault movement, mining operations, collapse of limestone caverns, or frost heave (in Northern climates).

Don't confuse settlement with subsidence—the compaction of subsurface soil layers, primarily sand and clay. That occurs over a broad area and at a relatively slow rate. The usual cause is the withdrawal of water (or oil or gas) from the sub-surface.

Most houses experience settlement within the first few years after construction, and usually it's no big deal. You will see settlement cracks in the foundation or house slab, masonry veneer, ceilings, or walls. (See Figure 23-3.) In severe cases, you may have trouble with windows, doors, and plumbing lines. Mechanical equipment may even be damaged.

Cracks may be structural and serious if they approach or exceed one-quarter inch in width, especially if they are growing larger. (See Figure 23-4.) Small hairline cracks may be due to minor settlement or to heat or moisture changes in construction materials.

Carefully check the inside and outside foundation walls. Up-and-down cracks may be acceptable, if they aren't wide and if the house isn't very new (five or fewer years old). But horizontal cracks can be scary: The ground may be pushing the walls in. A wall that bulges is also cause for alarm. (See Figures 23-3 and 23-4.)

Figure 23-3.   Foundation crack.

The foundation walls may be poured concrete (best), concrete blocks (second best), or cinder block. You can tell poured concrete from blocks that just have cement over them from the lines on the poured concrete. There are various foundation types. (See Figure 23-5.)

Prevention Measures

If the problem is clay soil that expands when it become wet, take the usual steps to keep water away from the foundation, such as putting splash blocks at the bottoms of downspouts, sloping the ground away from the foundation, or growing grass or other ground cover to absorb moisture. Also keep roots away from the foundation. During dry periods, soak the soil around the foundation (two to four feet away).

Corrective Measures

In extreme cases, extensive foundation work may be called for, such as excavating the soil below the foundation to pump in a special cement and soil mixture, to fill any voids. With slab settlement, reinforced concrete piers may have to be installed to a depth where the soil is stable. Such work is usually not only

Figure 23-4.   Serious vertical foundation crack.

very expensive, but can damage trees, lawns, and the interior plumbing. In many cases, there are less drastic solutions. If anyone tells you that your house needs foundation work, get a second opinion.

Red Flags

✔ The lighting in the basement is inadequate, and the steps are dangerous.

✔ The basement is damp and smelly.

✔ The floor is dirt, not concrete or concrete covered with tiles or linoleum.

✔ There are few windows, and small ones at that.

✔ There are rusty nails in the baseboard, watermarks on the

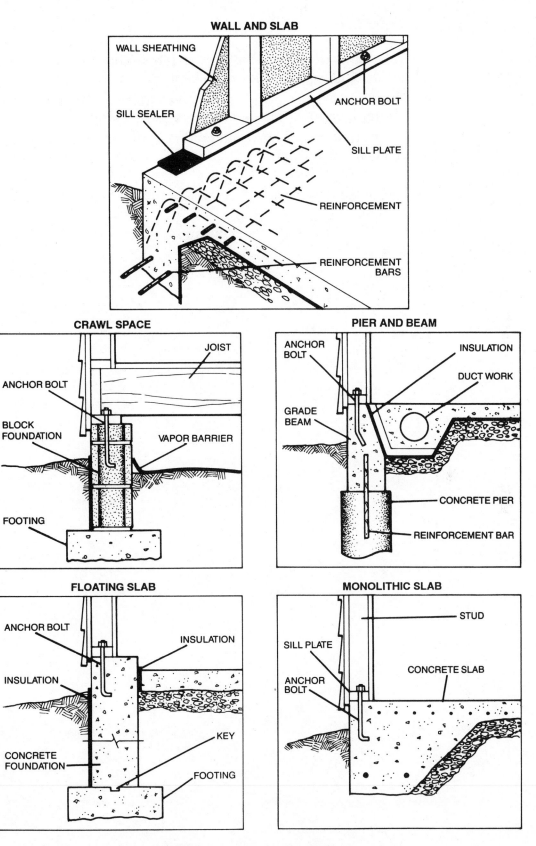

Figure 23-5.   Types of foundations.

walls, and rust at the bottom of the supporting beam. No books, clothes, or furniture are kept in the basement.

✔ There are cracks in foundation walls (or the slab) about a quarter inch in width, and they are getting larger.

✔ Cracks in walls are horizontal rather than vertical, indicating that that the wall may eventually fall down. Bulges in any wall are also worrisome.

✔ The neighbors have had serious settlement problems with their houses.

✔ There is evidence of carpenter ants (sawdust) or termites (mud tubes).

24

ELECTRICAL SYSTEMS

Besides binoculars, a screwdriver, and a tape measure, another vital piece of equipment you should have when you check out a house is an electrical outlet tester, available in any hardware store. It allows you to determine whether an outlet is functioning and whether it's grounded. Get one for 110/120-volt systems. Check every outlet in the house with your electrical tester. Also, turn every single light on or off.

Be especially careful when you check the electricity in older houses. Most houses over 40 years old probably have inadequate electrical capacity.

Many older houses have only two wires coming into a house, and a two-wire (110-volt), 60-ampere-rated electrical service entrance cable is inadequate. So are just four branch circuits to distribute the power. Such systems permit only basic lighting and a few appliances—theoretically, a maximum total power of about 7,000 watts. (See Figure 24-1.)

Another source of concern is that a standard home inspection does not include an evaluation of whether the electricity in a house satisfies the building codes. But many of the deficiencies noted in an inspection report are, in fact, code violations as well. If a house is relatively new or if there has been recent electrical work performed, ask the owners to document that the work was in compliance with the local electrical code.

DEFINITIONS

Let's pause for a few explanations:

Electricity is like water. Both are under pressure, have a rate of flow, and have some resistance.

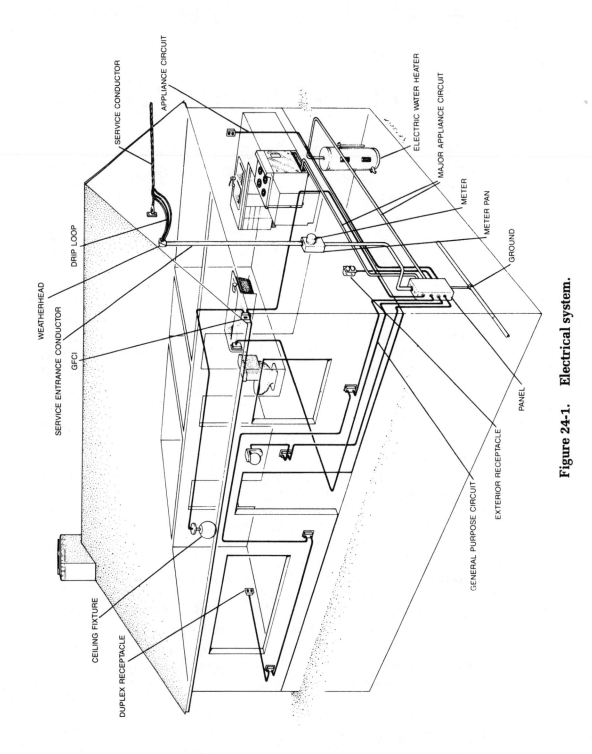

WEATHERHEAD

SERVICE ENTRANCE CONDUCTOR

GFCI

DRIP LOOP

SERVICE CONDUCTOR

APPLIANCE CIRCUIT

ELECTRIC WATER HEATER

MAJOR APPLIANCE CIRCUIT

METER

METER PAN

GROUND

PANEL

EXTERIOR RECEPTACLE

GENERAL PURPOSE CIRCUIT

CEILING FIXTURE

DUPLEX RECEPTACLE

Figure 24-1.   Electrical system.

The **electrical pressure** is measured in volts. Most house wiring has between 110 and 120 volts for lighting and small appliances. Only two wires are needed for a 120-volt system. For larger appliances like dryers, you need 230 to 240 volts. A 240-volt system that's grounded has three wires.

Rate of flow (current) is measured in amperes. A three-bedroom single-family house should have at least a 100-amp capacity.

Resistance or **friction** is measured in ohms. The larger a wire, and the shorter the wire, the lower its resistance.

Watts are a unit of electrical power. Wattage is calculated by multiplying the rate of flow of electricity (amps) by the volts (the force) (100 amps times 240 volts gives you 24,000 watts).

Power supply is usually measured in thousands of watts (kilowatts).

Pressure (force) is measured by volts. Volts = amperes × ohms

The **electrical service entrance** includes the system through which electricity enters the house: the service entrance wires, electric meter, main switch or circuit breaker, and main distribution or service panel. Branch circuits are the wires that carry electricity from the main service panel to lights, appliances, and electrical equipment.

Most electricity in this country is **alternative current** as opposed to **direct current**—it flows in one direction, then changes course, and back again.

A **convenience outlet** is for portable appliances, lamps, and kitchen appliances that don't require a lot of current, such as a refrigerator or microwave oven.

An **appliance outlet** is a three-wire outlet for large equipment like a range, dryer, or water heater. Such outlets operate on 240-volt current, with ratings of 30 to 50 amps. Only one major appliance should be used on each circuit.

Circuit breakers are protective devices that "trip" (turn off) to cut off the flow of electricity when the demand is greater than the main or branch circuits are designed to carry—in other words, when something is wrong. Unlike fuses, they need not be replaced if they trip. They must only be reset.

More old-fashioned are **fuses**, which snap or screw into position. When the ampere is excessive, a metal strip in the standard fuse melts and breaks the flow of electricity. Most fuses screw into their sockets; a cartridge type is used when more than 300 volts are in service.

The **main service panel** includes the main electrical shut-off switch and the panel box that houses the circuit breakers or fuses.

WIRING

Wires in a house may be numbered 10, 12, or 14. Number 10 wires are for large appliances requiring at least 220 volts (dryers, stoves, water heaters). Number 12 wires are for other appliances, which may be used more frequently, like toasters. Number 14 wires are for radios, alarm clocks, electric lights, and such.

Aluminum wiring is commonly used on main service lines and major appliance lines. While most worries relating to aluminum wiring focus on general-purpose house lines, you should have an electrician make a regular check of all connections whenever you know or suspect that there's aluminum wiring in a house. (More on aluminum wiring later.)

Knob-and-tube wiring is the original type of electrical wiring used in many homes. While it may work, it most likely has brittle insulation and doesn't have proper grounding. Expect to replace knob-and-tube wiring immediately or soon.

Low-voltage wiring uses safe, low-voltage power, usually for outside lighting systems. With time, low-voltage components need increased maintenance and may even fail.

Look at all exposed wires for fraying, especially the wires that leave the main panel. Is the insulation still fresh or is it brittle (old plastic) or soft (old cloth)?

A modern home needs a three-wire (220-volt) service entrance cable, especially for central air-conditioning and appliances like an electrical range, an oven, or a clothes dryer. (See Figure 24-2.)

The service lines can be buried or run overhead. Overhead lines should have adequate clearance over all points on the property and the house, so that you don't accidentally hit them with a pole or ladder.

When you're checking whether there are two or three wires coming into a house, examine the condition of the wires. Are they frayed? Are they accessible from a child's room? Are they near tree branches that might fall on them?

You should have 100 to 200 amps service. If you have a clothes washer or dryer, along with a variety of smaller appliances, you probably need at least 150 amps. The recommended service entrance capacity for the young, electronic household is 200 amps.

Combined lighting and appliances loads can run as high as 48,000 watts, which necessitates a large number and variety of branch circuits, each protected by an appropriate fuse or circuit breaker.

The panel box contains the connect between the power line and the house's wiring, the house circuit connections, the power cutoffs, and the overload protections (fuses or circuit breakers). All circuits

Figure 24-2.   Three-wire electrical service.

in the panel (including ground fault circuit interruptors) should be labeled, so that a particular circuit can be found in an emergency, or for servicing. (See Figure 24-3.) It's usually a good idea that there be one main cut-off to shut down a house's electrical system quickly and easily.

Inspect the fuse box or circuit breaker panel. You should have at least two 20-amp appliance circuits. The fuses or breakers should have ratings or 15 or 20 amps; if they're 25 or 30, they may be a fire hazard, especially in an older home where there hasn't been an electrical upgrading. (Exceptions: a fuse or breaker for the main service line coming into the house, or for a clothes dryer or other heavy appliance.)

Main panels often have multiple circuits connected to a single overload device. But this can be dangerous. It's better to have

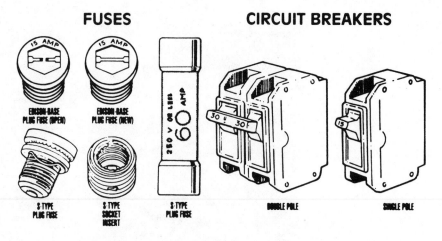

FUSES   **CIRCUIT BREAKERS**

Figure 24-3.   Fuses and circuit breakers.

only one circuit connected to an individual circuit breaker or fuse.

Visible rust in a panel indicates water or moisture penetration, and could mean hidden damage and a potential danger. Arrange an inspection by an electrician.

Here are the appropriate fuse or circuit breaker sizes for various appliances:

Appliance	Amps
Furnace	15
Dishwasher	20
Washing machine	20
Water heater	30
Clothes dryer	30
Electrical stove	50

Ground fault circuit interruptors are supersensitive circuit breakers. (See Figure 24-4.) They monitor the current flowing in the hot (black) and neutral (white) wires of a circuit. If the current flow in both wires is the same, everything is okay. But if more current flows in one wire than the other, some current must be grounded. A GFCI can sense any such imbalance and cut off power to the circuit within one-fortieth of a second.

GFCIs can save a person's life, especially if someone is standing on wet ground or in a damp bathroom. A wet body serves as a ready conductor of electricity. Rooms that should have GFCIs include

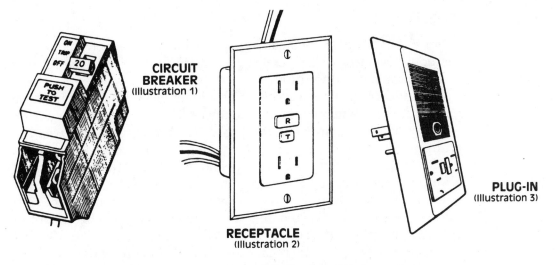

CIRCUIT
BREAKER
(Illustration 1)

PLUG-IN
(Illustration 3)

RECEPTACLE
(Illustration 2)

Figure 24-4.   Ground fault circuit interruptors.

bathrooms, kitchens, and sump pump installations. They are also called for on exterior wiring.

Three types of GFCIs are available:

1. A replacement for your present circuit breakers in your panel box;

2. A replacement for an outlet in a critical location; and

3. A portable GFCI.

Grounding and Polarity

A house should have a continuous electrical grounding from all points in the system, so that excess electricity can be discharged into the ground. From the panel, a large wire should disappear into the ground or be attached to a metal plumbing pipe.

Electrical receptacles (two prong) that aren't grounded shouldn't be used with certain appliances, or—if they are—they must be used with a three-prong adapter, where the third prong is for grounding. In some situations, rewiring the circuits may be necessary to provide a continuous ground.

Does every outlet in the house have a third receptable for three-prong plugs? If it's a two-slot receptable, check that the screw—to which you would attach the free wire from a prong—is grounded. Touch a wire from your tester to the screw and the other wire to each of the two slots. The tester will glow when you hit a "hot" wire (unless the outlet is dead or the screw has been painted over).

Aluminum Wiring

From about 1965 to 1973, many home builders, electricians, and remodelers switched from copper wiring in general-purpose circuits to less expensive aluminum.

Soon electrical fires and other problems began to occur in these buildings with increasing frequency. Although improper wiring techniques caused some of the problems, the main cause was the aluminum connections, particularly on general-purpose circuits.

The basic problem was the special physical characteristics of aluminum. Aluminum has a greater resistance to current flow than copper has, so aluminum wire was made larger. Aluminum also oxidizes more quickly, so bare aluminum should have been kept to a minimum throughout a system. Aluminum also expands and contracts faster, which increases the chances of connections loosening. It's less elastic, too, making it more likely to be damaged if handled improperly.

The most serious deficiency of household aluminum wiring is the development of a gap between the wire and the device connectors as the wire expands and contracts with frequent use. This gap leads to the arcking of the electric circuit between the wire and the connectors—in other words, to sparks. This could ignite adjacent materials.

Also common is the overheating of the wire because of corrosion from the contact of two dissimilar metals, or because of the oxidation of the exposed aluminum at a connection. Either condition leads to greater resistance and sometimes to fire.

The worst problem areas are the switches and receptacles used most often or that have a lot of current flowing through them. The on-off frequency of these devices, especially in kitchens and bathrooms, speeds up the failure of the device itself or other connections on the same circuit.

Signs of danger with aluminum wiring include:

- Coverplates that are hot to the touch;
- Flickering lights;
- Sporadic appliance operation;
- Scorch marks around outlets;
- Inoperative receptacles or switches; and
- The smell of burning plastic.

In 1972 manufacturers changed both aluminum wire and electrical devices to improve the systems. But the problems continued, and the old type of aluminum wiring was still sold after 1972.

Since then, various procedures have been used to lessen the dangers of aluminum—short of rewiring an entire house, the cost of which could be enormous. These efforts lowered but did not eliminate all risk.

Since 1973 the use of aluminum wire in household circuits has dwindled tremendously. But aluminum on the main service line into a house panel and on major appliance circuits continues in many areas of the country. The danger with such connections can be minimized if the proper installations are made and maintenance precautions are observed.

Today the consensus is that all aluminum wire systems should be checked by an electrician periodically (and before a closing), to determine whether any danger exists. Systems that have not been upgraded should be evaluated on what steps might be taken and what the cost might be.

Red Flags

- ✔ Only two wires come into the house, providing 110-volt, 60-ampere-rated electrical service.
- ✔ There's aluminum wiring in a house.
- ✔ Exposed wiring is frayed.
- ✔ You don't have at least two 20-amp appliance circuits.
- ✔ The control panel has rusty areas.
- ✔ Electrical grounding isn't available throughout the house.
- ✔ Many extension cords and octopus plugs are in use.
- ✔ Electrical plugs have black areas—a sign of a previous short-circuit.
- ✔ The owners report that fuses blow or breakers trip frequently.
- ✔ Lights often go dim.
- ✔ Stairways and entrances are unlit or dimly lit.
- ✔ The outlets near bathing and washing areas don't have GFCIs.
- ✔ You must grope in the dark for light switches. (The switches should have built-in lights.)

25

HEATING
AND AIR-CONDITIONING

Whether gas or oil heat is more expensive depends on your particular area, but electrical heat is almost always the most costly. Still, builders like electrical heating because it's easy to install, it burns cleanly, and it can be regulated for individual rooms.

Heat is usually distributed by water, air, or steam. Water and steam remain in radiators longer, keeping rooms at an even temperature. With warm-air heat, the results are more immediate, but the hot air being delivered is very dry, hence the need for the addition of moisture to the air by way of a humidifier. When the furnace is on, it delivers warm air (usually around 110 degrees Fahrenheit), but there's little residual heat, as with hot-water and steam systems. The cycles of warm-air heat may make room temperatures fluctuate. A solution is to keep the furnace blower fan on continuous air circulation.

The ducts used with warm-air may be adaptable for central air-conditioning, provided that the system has the proper air returns and a high-volume blower fan. Also, with warm-air systems, you can filter the air to some degree.

In inspecting either a furnace (hot-air) or boiler (steam or water), turn up the thermostat to activate the system. The furnace should respond promptly, but allow an hour or more to feel the results from a boiler system: It takes time for the heated water or steam to reach all of the radiators or baseboard units. Check all rooms for a heat source and comfort levels. (Many finished basements and attics have heating deficiencies.)

The area around a furnace or boiler should be fireproof (for example, no wooden beams nearby).

There should be at least one heat source for every outside wall in each room.

WARM-AIR HEATING

The most common type of heating systems in houses today are warm-air furnaces, which use either gas, oil, or electricity as fuel. (See Figure 25-1.) Most systems installed since the 1950s are power-driven by blower fans: They don't rely on gravity to distribute the heated air throughout the house.

Here's how they work. Air from the house enters the furnace, where a filter or electronic air cleaner traps airborne dirt. A blower forces the air up into a compartment called a heat exchanger, which

Figure 25-1.   Warm-air furnace.   **Figure 25-2.   Warm-air furnace ready for inspection.**

contains metal passageways heated to temperatures of several hundred degrees by burning gases. The passageway exteriors heat the air as the blower forces it past and into the network of ducts that go throughout the house. A fan control switches the blower on and off, and shuts down the blower if the temperature of the circulating air rises too high.

Forced warm-air systems heat uniformly, with register temperatures around 110 degrees Fahrenheit. They can respond rapidly to changes in temperature.

One way to check the furnace is to watch its ignition. (See Figure 25-2.) Remove the front panel(s) and have someone turn up the thermostat. When it lights, listen for unusual noises. Make sure that smoke isn't coming into the basement and that you can't smell the combustion—a sign of a crack. Another sign is a dancing or flickering flame pattern at the burners. Listen for the fan to come on when the furnace becomes warm.

Registers will supply the heat, and grilles will return the cool air. The registers should be on the outside walls, the grilles on the inside walls. Dark stains on the registers may be a sign of a malfunction in the heating system. The registers should be adjustable, so you can alter the air supply to various sections or rooms in the house.

In houses with only a central return register, the blower fan should run continuously to improve air circulation and reduce drafts.

Thermostats operate the central heating system and help keep the house at an even temperature. Be sure that the thermostats are properly positioned. Those placed in cold hallways or hot kitchens won't see to it that balanced heat is distributed throughout the house. To save fuel, an automatic setback (dual is best) thermostat is desirable. This automatically turns a system on and off at specific times and temperatures. (See Figure 25-3.)

Figure 25-3.   Dual setback thermostat.

Contrary to popular belief, turning up a thermostat doesn't raise the temperature of the air entering a room through the registers. Instead, it just signals the furnace to continue pumping the standard degree of heated air into the room for a longer time, until the desired room temperature is reached.

The best advice is to either use your preset setback thermostat (which lowers and raises the setting at predetermined times), or to select a particular temperature and leave it alone. If you feel a chill, put on a sweater or whatever to warm your extremities (which feel cold first).

The ultimate energy waster in a warm-air system is a dirty air filter. The system must labor hard to pump the air through such an obstruction.

Ideally, the homeowner will have had a utility or dealer provide annual system inspection and maintenance.

Gas-fired furnaces have pilot lights that should be left burning to prevent rust and condensation on heat-exchanger surfaces. Keeping the pilot lights on also avoids delays when you want to start the system in chilly weather. The furnace should also have a safety device to cut off the gas supply if the pilot light goes out. (Newer furnaces use electronic ignition, with no pilot light.)

A serious threat to a heat exchanger is a leaky humidifier mounted above the furnace, causing the exchanger to rust and eventually to

Figure 25-4.   Humidifier mounted over furnace.

fail. Thanks to rust, some exchangers have failed after only 5 years—when their expected life spans are 12 to 18 years. And usually the replacement of a heat exchanger means that the entire furnace must be replaced.

Automatic humidifiers drive homeowners crazy. Rarely do they work satisfactorily for extended periods of time, especially in areas where the water is hard. Many homeowners content themselves with just room humidifiers, or leave water available to evaporate in the winter. (See Figure 25-4.)

Hot Water and Steam

A steam system contains air, not just water, and it has a water-level gauge. Radiators in the rooms will have escape valves, to let hot air escape and the steam rise. (See Figures 25-5 and 25-6.)

Check the boiler for cracks and leaks. The water level (in the boiler) in the gauge glass should be about midway up. If the water in the gauge seems dirty or if the level fluctuates a lot, the boiler should be serviced. Also make sure there's a low water cutoff (which shuts down the unit if the water level drops too low).

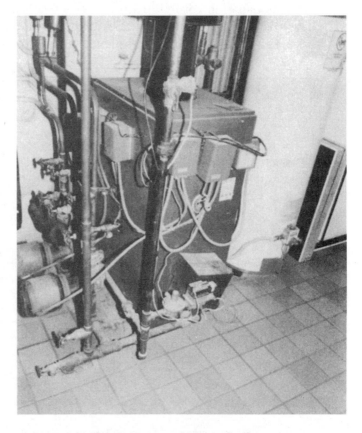

Figure 25-5.   Steam boiler.

Figure 25-6.   Steam radiator.

Hot-water systems should work ideally by pumps, not by gravity. All units installed in the past 40 years are powered. (See Figure 25-7.) Heat is delivered throughout the house to room radiators or baseboard units. (See Figure 25-8.)

Check the pipes and nearby areas for rust and stains. If there's a clamp over a pipe, it's a sign that at least one area has leaked.

HEAT PUMPS

A heat pump is sort of a reverse-flow air conditioner. If you turned your room air conditioner around in the winter months, it would extract heat from the outside air and pump it into the inside.

A heat pump is different from the usual central heating or cooling systems. Among the differences:

- **Lower temperature air**—During the heating season, the heat pump circulates a large amount of lower-temperature air than you may be used to. The register temperature of a warm-air furnace is in the 110–120 degree Fahrenheit range. A heat pump delivers air temperature in the 90–95 degree Fahrenheit range—warm, but when felt directly at the register on 98.6 degree Fahrenheit skin, the air seems cool.

Figure 25-7.   Hot water boiler.

- **Defrost cycle**—In humid weather with near-freezing temperatures, frost may form on a heat pump's outdoor coil. Like a modern refrigerator, the heat pump defrosts itself automatically. It does this by switching to the cooling mode, which pumps hot gas through the outdoor coil, melting the ice.
- **Failure to operate**—If the pump doesn't go on, check fuses or circuit breakers to make sure the power is on.
- **Emergency heat switch**—In normal operation, the compressor continues to run as the outdoor temperature decreases. In the event of a heat pump breakdown, a manually operated switch permits the resistance heaters to provide emergency heat.
- **Completely automatic**—If you set the heating and cooling temperatures just once, your house will remain comfortable. On a hot day, the cooling cycle cools the house. If the outside

Figure 25-8.   Baseboard hot-water unit.

temperature drops sufficiently overnight, the heating cycle will begin.

- **Outdoor thermostat**—In addition to an indoor thermostat, if you have one or more preset outdoor thermostats, you will only rarely have to use extra heat. By controlling the successive "come-on" stages of the expensive resistance heat as the outdoor temperature drops to different levels, you raise the efficiency of the system.

- **Compressor warning indicator**—Some manufacturers install built-in warning circuits to alert you if the compressor fails. Without this warning, you may not discover the failure until you get your electric bill.

- **Supply air registers**—Any reduction in indoor air flow will affect a heat pump's operation and could damage the compressor. That's why you should not close more than one register in your home at any one time. Don't block the air register with furniture or drapes. In fact, it's a good idea to keep the fan switch in the "on" position. A heat pump's low air-velocity design relies on continuous fan operation to avoid different air temperatures in certain portions of your house.

Here's how a heat pump works. The heat pump's compressor pumps a refrigerant (a cooling gas, usually Freon) between the indoor and outdoor coils, carrying heat from one place to another. The refrigerant changes back and forth between a liquid and a gas, depending on which part of the operating cycle it's in. Electric blower-fans keep the air moving across these coils, and thus circulate cool or warm air throughout your house.

During the summer, the heat pump works like any conventional air conditioner. A cool refrigerant gas absorbs heat from the air inside your house. Air passing over the coils circulates and cools your house. The refrigerant is transferred to the outside coil, where it gives up its heat, becomes cool, and turns into a liquid. The refrigerant is then pumped through an expansion device into the indoor coil, where once again it becomes a cool gas. Then the cycle starts again.

The heat pump is "turned around" from its cooling cycle by a special valve that reverses the flow of refrigerant through the system. When that happens, the operation of the indoor and outdoor coils and fans is reversed, so that the outdoor coil picks up the heat and the indoor coil releases the heat.

During the winter, the refrigerant in the outdoor coil is a low-temperature gas that is much colder than outdoor temperatures and, therefore, absorbs heat from winter air. (There is heat—measured in British Thermal Units—in sub-zero air; 82 percent of the heating BTUs at 100 degrees Fahrenheit are still available at 0 degrees Fahrenheit.)

The compressor pressurizes this heat-laden gas and pumps it through the indoor coil. As air is blown over the coils, the high-pressure gas gives off the heat it collected outside. The warm air then circulates to heat your house. As the refrigerant gas gives up its heat and cools, it condenses into a liquid and is pumped back to the outdoor coil, where it changes once again into its gaseous form to repeat the cycle. (See Figure 25-9.)

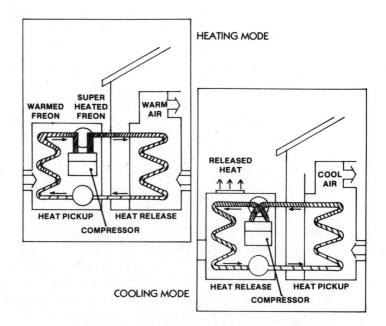

Figure 25-9.   Diagram of heat pump system.

Several heat pump manufacturers now offer dual compressor models, which operate more efficiently at lower temperatures. At temperatures where conventional heat pumps switch to the more costly resistance heat, these newer models turn to their second compressors, designed to extract further BTUs from the outdoor air. (See Figure 25-10.)

Another innovation is the heat pump water heater. It's available in various models, such as a self-contained tank and heat pump unit. Another is a remote system for retrofitting into an existing water tank. Yet another one is installed in an existing heat pump or air conditioner, to tap any discharged heat.

AIR CONDITIONING

Most central air-conditioning systems are the electrical-compressor type. Others include the gas absorption system, the chilled water system, and the evaporative cooling system (lovingly referred to as a "swamp cooler").

Electrical systems come in two flavors:

- The single package type, with the entire system within the house; and

Figure 25-10.   Dual heat pumps.

- The split system, in which the condensor/compressor is outside the house. (See Figure 25-11.)

Normally, a central air can be expected to last from five to eight years. Usually it's the compressor that goes first, and, naturally, it's the most expensive part of the system. Replacement compressors have an even shorter life span than the originals because they can become contaminated during shipping and installation.

Central air is much more convenient than window air-conditioning units. You don't have to keep adjusting window units throughout the house, and it's not sweltering when you walk into a room that's not cooled. A house without window units is also more attractive from the outside. Quieter, too. On the other hand, window units can be more economical: You're not cooling the entire house. Also, if the central air shuts off, your house may become temporarily uninhabitable.

When purchasing a room air conditioner, look for one that's the right size. Don't be tempted to buy one that's oversized. Not only will you waste energy, but you will experience the "cave effect." That's when your super-sized unit will bring the room temperature

Figure 25-11.   Air conditioning compressor.

down before it has time to bring the humidity down: The air is cool but damp—as in a cave.

Air-conditioning removes heat from the air inside and releases it outside. It cools because a gas that's expanding gathers heat; a gas turning into a liquid releases heat. In a system, a liquid—called the refrigerant (usually Freon)—expands into a gas, thus absorbing heat from the air. The cooled air is then circulated through ducts into the area to be cooled. The compressor, a mechanical pump, then forces the gas back into a liquid again, releasing heat.

To test a system: If the temperature is above 60 degrees Fahrenheit, turn the system on and check the temperatures in individual rooms. Ideally, the temperature at the room registers should be around 55 degrees Fahrenheit. Also check the operation of the thermostat.

If the outside temperature is below 60 degrees Fahrenheit, don't turn on the system: Running a system in such cool weather can damage the compressor. Instead, ask the owners about the system; ask for the name of the service company and the date of the last servicing. (A system should be checked once a year.)

Check that the ducts that pass through hot areas like attics, garages, and crawl spaces are well insulated.

Make sure that windows and doors are properly weather-stripped, to minimize the infiltration of hot air.

If there's a drain pan under the unit, as is the case in many attic installations, make sure the pan is clear and the condensate drain is open. (The condensate is the water removed from the air.) If your unit has a condensate pump, check that it's clean and working. See that the inlets and outlets, indoors and outdoors, are free of dust and other obstructions; otherwise, the system's life expectancy may be unusually short.

If there's no lock on the outside electrical disconnect box, add one. Otherwise, mischievous children may damage the system.

Red Flags

- ✔ The furnace or boiler doesn't come on quickly.
- ✔ Some rooms remain chilly while others are warm.
- ✔ There's a leaky humidifier above the furnace.
- ✔ The furnace doesn't have a safety device to cut off the gas supply if the pilot light goes out.
- ✔ A boiler has cracks and leaks. The water level is low or high, or dirty, or fluctuates. There's no low water cutoff to shut down the unit if the water level drops too low.
- ✔ Pipes and nearby areas have rust and stains. There's a clamp over a pipe, an indication that it leaked.
- ✔ There's no heat source in every living area.

OIL OR GAS HEAT?

Oil-heated houses are common mainly in the Northeast, and even there their number is dwindling. By and large, gas is the fuel of choice. If you're undecided about which of two or three houses to buy, other things being equal, choose the one heated by gas, not oil or electricity (which is expensive).

In 1980, some 42,658,000 housing units in this country had utility gas heat, according to the Bureau of the Census. In 1987, the latest year for which data are available, 45,959,000 units had gas—a 7.7 percent increase. In 1980, some 14,655,000 units had oil or kerosene. In 1987, the figure had dropped to 13,813,000—a 5.7 percent decrease.

Almost all new homes have gas or electricity, not oil. In fact, more homes are now heated by electricity than by oil.

The case for gas:

- Gas burns cleaner.
- Gas burners are more maintenance-free than oil burners. Also, oil burners lose their efficiency faster than gas burners.
- Supplies of gas are more reliable.

Says one heating contractor, "Oil is overpriced, it's noisy, and it smells." You also don't have to worry about your oil tank leaking and polluting the ground, which could cost you thousands of dollars in cleanup expenses.

One utility, PSE&G in New Jersey, claims that customers who have recently converted from oil enjoyed yearly fuel savings of 10 percent to 40 percent. According to Public Service, homeowners prefer natural gas, and natural gas enhances the value of a house.

Not that there are no arguments for oil. The Consumer Energy Council of the American Research Foundation in Washington, D.C., states in its literature: "For the 95 percent of consumers who do not need a new furnace, conversion makes no economic sense." Converting to gas, it claims, is "a bad investment."

An oil supplier adds, "I'm not claiming that gas will blow you up or asphyxiate you [yes, he is], but it's comforting to know that oil can't do those things."

As for the comparative costs of the two fuels, the oil industry argues that despite oil's volatility, over the years the prices tend to be close.

Isn't the supply of gas more reliable? "Gas isn't the magic bullet," says David Moreland, a spokesman for the Petroleum Marketers of America in Washington, D.C. "Gas resources are good, but not infinite, and if many people convert, there may be a supply problem."

Aren't oil burners noisier? Replies an oil man, "It's like an air conditioner going on and off. It's not a major factor." Aren't gas burners cleaner? Says our oil man, "Both oil and gas are clean if the burners are properly maintained."

Still, the consensus among independent experts seems to be that gas is a better choice. Homeowners with older, inefficient oil systems who can afford the cost of conversion should think of switching, especially when their current oil burners conk out. And, as mentioned, buyers should veer toward houses with gas heating.

THE COST OF CONVERTING

Replacing an oil burner with a gas burner may cost $1,800 to $2,800. The price includes the installation of an automatic day-night thermostat, and filling the old storage tank with sand (if it's buried outside) or cutting it up and carrying it away (if it's inside the house). About half of all houses with oil heat have outside tanks, half inside. Oil burners with outside, buried tanks are more expensive to replace because of the expense of digging and the possibility of soil contamination (a monster expense).

Replacing a steam system is the most expensive, then hydronic (water) systems, then hot-air systems. Charges may be higher if gas pipes are not already feeding into the house (for cooking) or if the utility feed lines are far away.

Before converting, a homeowner should either (1) notify his or her oil company not to fill the tank, and wait until it's nearly empty, or (2) hire a company to pump out and buy the oil remaining in the tank. In any case, the soil around the tank should be checked.

A conversion typically takes two days. Get two estimates from heating contractors, and run their names past the Better Business Bureau.

=== 27 ===

WATER PENETRATION, PLUMBING, AND SEWAGE

Water can be friendly (when it's available on call at your kitchen or bathroom tap or fixture) or unfriendly (when it enters your house uninvited and surreptitiously). Most instances of wet basements, garages, crawl spaces, and so forth can be remedied with minimum effort and expense. So they aren't necessarily a reason to reject a house, if the price is right and you obtain adequate safeguards.

Most water penetration occurs because its major causes (rainwater from the roof, surface water from rain, melting snow or ice) are not dealt with, and water accumulates around the house and eventually seeps in. But each house varies, so a special plan of attack should be developed for each.

You must deal with the cause of the penetration, not the effect. Many homeowners will find a way to handle the water after it has entered (effect), rather than stopping it in the first place (cause).

The best way to determine the cause of water penetration is to walk around the house after a heavy rainfall of several hours. Check how the gutters and downspouts are handling the roof run off. If there are no gutters, find out where the roof runoff is accumulating. Also see if there is a flow of surface water toward the house. Armed with this basic information, consider the following advice on causes and solutions.

CAUSES

The most common causes of water penetration are:

1. Rainwater funneled down the downspout exits at the foundation, where it accumulates and seeps through cracks in walls, doorways, windows, and window wells.
2. The property is flat or slopes toward the house, permitting surface water to collect and drain down against the foundation walls.
3. The original house plan and workmanship may have been faulty.
4. There's street runoff down the driveway.
5. There aren't enough gutters or downspouts to handle the roof water, or those that are there are defective. The free-falling water forms puddles and erodes the soil near the foundation.
6. Areaway drains are clogged, and they are not covered.
7. Condensation (sweating) of atmospheric moisture on cool surfaces (walls, floors, water pipes) causes water to build up.
8. The subsurface or groundwater level (water table) is close to the level of the crawl space or basement, or even above the level.
9. In rare cases, water from natural springs flows below the house throughout the year, or only during periods of heavy rainfall.

Solutions—Minor Problems

Start with these inexpensive remedies first.

1. Make sure that the gutters aren't clogged and leaking. Be certain that all downspouts are clear, and end in a splash block, which will disperse the water. If possible, pipe the water to the curb or to a storm sewer or a lower place on the property. Drywells, as they are called, tend to clog up unless they are very large and continue to drain properly.
2. Check any underground lines. They tend to clog up and should be checked regularly in season.
3. Be certain that window wells are clean, are of the proper height, and have plastic covers to shed water. Areaways should be covered and have a working drain.
4. Hook up a dehumidifier and run it during the damp season.
5. Install a berm at the end of the driveway to minimize street runoff water. (A berm is a built-up lip of asphalt or concrete that diverts water. See Figure 27-1.)

Figure 27-1.   Berm at end of sloping driveway.

6.   Raise the grade of the soil next to the house to a slope of about 15 degrees. Don't raise the grade very close to the siding or above it.

7.   Encourage a good growth of grass, and grade the entire lot slightly to direct water away from the house.

8.   Install a sump pit and pump at the lowest level of the basement, and divert the water it catches away from the foundation.

If the water penetration subsides after you have taken any of these steps, then coat the interior walls with waterproof paint. First clean the walls of efflorescence, mildew, peeling paint, and so forth, and seal all joints, cracks, and holes with a waterproof caulk. The paint won't hold back water, but it will help control dampness. (Efflorescence is the white powder that forms on the surface of masonry when moisture leaches through.)

Solutions—Major Problems

You may have major problems if:

•   The house is on the side of a hill;

•   Surface water tends to form ponds;

- The soil is permeable, but only slowly;
- The house is in a marshy area;
- The rains have raised the normal water table; or
- The house is at the bottom of a steep driveway. (See Figure 27-2.)

Here are additional steps to consider:

1. To control excess runoff, especially on the side of a hill, develop a thick turf, terrace the slopes to slow the runoff, and dig a swale (a depression in the earth) around the house, at least ten feet away.
2. Install subsurface drains or ditches to channel off the water.
3. If the water table is high, have the exterior around the foundation dug up. Seal the walls, and install drain tile below the floor to collect and divert the water to a sump pit or away from the foundation.

Of course, be sure to obtain several estimates on any repairs.

Figure 27-2.   Driveway sloped toward house.

PRIVATE WATER SYSTEMS

Wells, cisterns, and springs provide water for about 20 percent of the homes in the United States and service over 40 million Americans. Wells are the most common.

The fresh water that's the source of most wells is *groundwater*. This is the word describing rain, snow, and other precipitation that seeps into the ground and percolates down to a saturated layer of sand, gravel, or rock. The top surface of this water is known as the *water table*.

Ask the sellers for all available information on the system—plot plan, past service record, water source, and so forth. Talk with municipal officers about local water and well conditions. Order a laboratory analysis of the water.

Water Quality

As water percolates through the ground, it becomes purified, although it can pick up minerals and other pollutants as well. In general, deeper wells provide better-quality water because of this filtering.

When you purchase a house with a private well system, your mortgage lender may require that you have the water analyzed. The quality of the water should never be taken for granted. If you're just having a well installed, have the water analyzed at the time of installation and every so often afterwards.

Water Testing

A potability test will determine if the water contains any dangerous bacteria. That's the minimum testing requirement. But pay for a complete water analysis—you also want to know about excessive mineral content, hardness, acidity, and chemical contamination.

Types of Wells

Shallow wells draw water from less than 25 feet below ground level. Deep wells tend to have safer water, but the greater depth makes it more difficult to draw up the water.

Types of Pumps

The three basic types of pumps are submersible, jet, and piston. All three can be used for shallow or deep wells, but the submersible pump is most suitable for deep wells.

The piston pump is a descendant of the old hand pump, and it's not in general use today.

The jet pump has two parts: a jet assembly and a certifugal pump. The pump is like a small water wheel, driven by a motor. This wheel increases the speed and the pressure of the water, diverting part of it to the jet assembly.

The jet assembly has no moving parts, but uses this recirculated water to create a suction that draws well water into the assembly and pushes this water back to the pump. The water passes through the pump, and part of it is circulated again and part sent on to the house's water system.

A submersible pump is located inside the well, and the electrical motor and centrifugal pump are both designed to operate under water. Because the pump is inside the well, water is drawn in through screened openings and is pumped up through a single discharge pipe. Although this type of pump is difficult to service, it works quietly and in very deep wells.

How They Work

If a system consisted only of the pipes and the pump, the pump would have to operate every time someone filled a glass with water or flushed a toilet. This would result in excessive wear and a premature failure of the pump. That's why the system has a storage or "pressure" tank to hold water. (See Figure 27-3.)

This tank is partially filled with air. As the pump forces water into the tank, the air is compressed. This compressed air forces water through the household pipes whenever a faucet or valve is opened. As the water leaves the storage tank, the air inside expands and the pressure decreases. When the pressure in the tank drops, the pump goes up and starts forcing water into the tank until the pressure increases. A gauge in the system indicates the current pressure.

A pressure switch in the system senses the pressure and activates the pump at the proper time. This switch is usually adjustable, with an average preset start/stop pressure of about 30 to 50 pounds per square inch (psi).

To check a well, run the water for a period of time, then examine the water tank and controls for leaks, making sure that everything is operating smoothly.

The storage tank's pressure gauge should have a maximum pressure of 75 psi. The pressure switch brings in water when the pressure drops below a certain level. You might test the switch by turning on a faucet and watching the needle on the gauge fall. Then listen for the click as the automatic switch goes on.

Signs of Trouble

You will have a waterlogged tank when the air inside is slowly absorbed into the water. This causes the pressure to change rapidly as the water enters or leaves the tank. So the pump begins cycling

Figure 27-3.   Well water tank.

(starting and stopping frequently). The antidote is to introduce more air into the tank.

Another problem is condensation. Well water is usually 52 degrees to 55 degrees Fahrenheit, so water vapor may condense inside the warmer tank and inside the pipes. To minimize sweating and dripping and to prevent rust, insulate on the tank and the pipes that are affected.

Hot-Water Heaters

Most hot-water heaters are either gas- or electric-powered self-standing units. Some homes have water heating coils (instantaneous hot water system) built into the heating system's boiler. These often fail to provide an adequate supply of hot water.

A problem to be alert for is if the cold water enters the gas or electric heater at the top instead of at the bottom. As the cold water works its way down, it will absorb the heat—and you'll wind up reducing the life of the heater by four or five years. (See Figures 27-4 and 27-5.)

Another sign of trouble is when the flame goes out regularly. The cause may be a leak, and that means the heater must be repaired. Leaks cannot be repaired.

Replace a hot water heater before it fails. If it bursts, 50 gallons of hot water can do a lot of damage. (See Figure 27-6.)

A gas water heater should have a minimal capacity of 50 gallons for a family of five, 40 for a family of four, and 30 for a family of three. Electric units should have a minimum 50-gallon capacity. Water heaters usually have a life of at least ten years. Determine when a heater was installed; the date may be on the heater itself. Look for rust on the heater's seams. Also, check how quickly the water in a house gets hot.

Figure 27-4.   Gas hot-water heater.

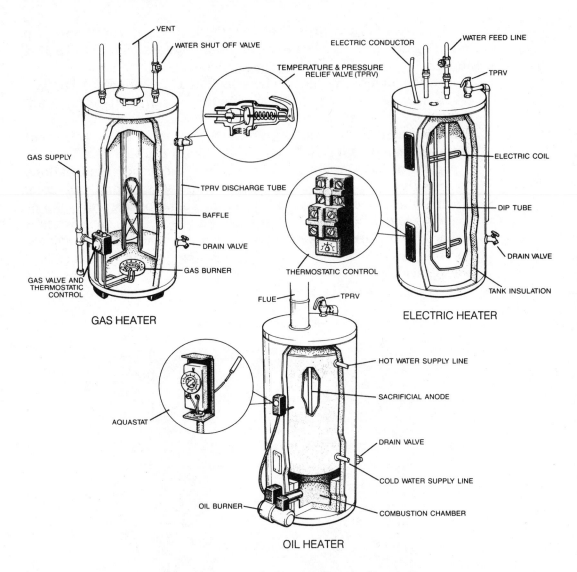

Figure 27-5.   Diagrams of water heaters.

PLUMBING

Check the water pressure in the house. In a bathroom, turn on the shower and run a bath; then flush a toilet. See if the water flow to the bathtub slows down a lot. This could mean that your water piping is clogged with mineral buildup, and you may have to replace certain sections. But before agreeing to such an expensive job, have the plumber check the pressure-reducing valve near the water supply entry point to be house. It could be set at too low a pressure. (See Figure 27-7.)

Galvanized iron pipes, which you can identify because a magnet is attracted to them, are probably 60 years old now and nearing the

Figure 27-6.   Pressure-relief valve on water heater.

end of their life expectancy. They should be replaced, especially if the water is rusty or the water flow is restricted.

Brass pipes, which look like iron, are also probably 50 to 60 years old and are ready to give up the ghost. Check the joints for water drips and for the blue color of copper oxide, a sign of deterioration. Look at the bottom of the pipes for pinholes, which may be letting out lime or water vapor. Because brass is brittle, you cannot replace only bad sections. You will have to replace entire lines.

Copper lines, the most common, also wear out in about 50 to 75 years. Check the fittings for seepage.

You may have a special problem if the pipes in your house are made of different metals. They may interact chemically (galvanic action). An "ion trap" (a device that prevents chemical interactions) may be the answer. If the pipes are made of different metals—copper here, galvanized iron there—it's a sign that the owner has been replacing them. Further replacements may be needed soon.

The longest-lived pipes are made of copper or brass, not galvanized iron. But the line connecting the house drainage pipes to the main sewer should be iron. As for the new plastic pipes, they are considered the low-priced spread—cheap and breakable. Lead pipes may be a health hazard. To identify such pipes, scratch them with a screwdriver. You may see the shiny gray color of the lead.

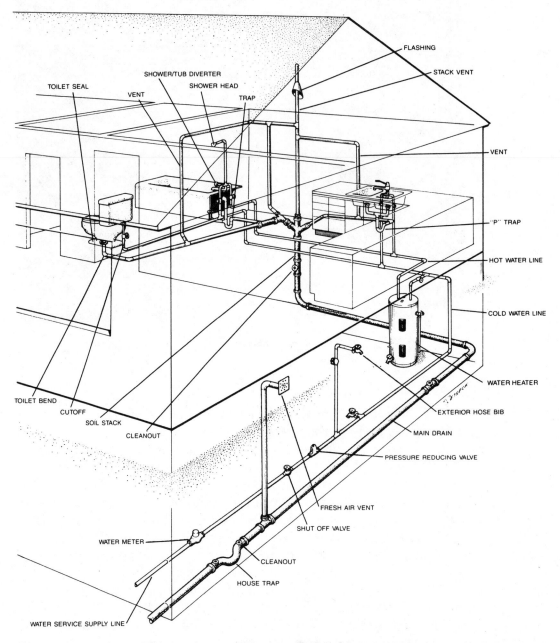

Figure 27-7.   Diagram of plumbing system.

The best pipe systems in general are the most direct, with the fewest sharp angles. Ideally, drainage pipes will have cleanouts, where you can get access to a pipe that is clogged up.

Examine the area around and below water pipes for wet spots on the ceiling, floors, and walls. Check the pipes themselves for rust, mineral deposits, wetness, or discoloration. There should be no sagging in horizontal pipes. All sinks, toilets, and other fixtures should have turnoff knobs underneath, so you can make repairs without switching off the water at the main line.

Red Flags

Water Penetration Anywhere in the House

- ✔ The house is on the side of a hill or at the bottom of a steep driveway.
- ✔ Surface water tends to form ponds.
- ✔ The soil is permeable, but only slowly.
- ✔ The house is in a marshy area.
- ✔ You see damp spots in the basement, or smell mildew.
- ✔ You see that nails in the basement floorboard are rusty, and there are watermarks on the walls.
- ✔ There aren't enough gutters and downspouts around a house.
- ✔ When you visit after a rainfall, the gutters and downspouts seem to be clogged up.
- ✔ Rainwater coming down the leader exits at the foundation, where it accumulates.
- ✔ The property is flat or slopes toward the house, permitting surface water to collect and drain against the foundation walls.

Private Water Systems

- ✔ The owners cannot provide you with much data (plot plan, record of service, and so forth).
- ✔ Municipal officers are not encouraging about local water and well conditions.
- ✔ You run the water for a period of time, and find leaks and hear unexpected noises.
- ✔ Your well is deep, but you don't have a submersible pump.
- ✔ The well starts pumping quickly and stopping quickly.
- ✔ Not enough water is produced for your family.

Hot Water Heaters

- ✔ The cold water enters the heater at the top instead of at the bottom.
- ✔ The pilot light goes out regularly.
- ✔ There isn't enough capacity for your family.
- ✔ The water becomes hot slowly.

✔ There's rust on the heater's seams.

✔ The heater is over 15 years old.

Plumbing

✔ There are wet spots on the ceiling, floors, and walls.

✔ The pipes themselves have rust, mineral deposits, wetness, or discoloration.

✔ The pipes are made of galvanized iron and the water is rusty.

✔ The pipes are made of brass, and you see water drips at the joints, the blue color of copper oxide, and pinholes at the bottom of the pipes.

✔ The pipes in your house are made of different metals and may interact chemically.

✔ The pipes are made of lead—a possible health hazard.

✔ The drainage pipes don't have cleanouts.

✔ The pipes have sharp angles, and therefore may clog up.

✔ The waste lines in the basement are up high. (You will need special ejector pumps to drain any fixtures.)

✔ You see lead solder joints and fittings.

=== 28 ===

EXAMINING A SEPTIC SYSTEM

As much as 25 percent of the nation's population lives in residences that use septic systems to dispose of household waste. Yet some people whose houses have such systems have no idea what they are—until a plumber explains why something has gone wrong with the plumbing.

Septic systems are concentrated in suburban or rural areas. Here's how they work. Household waste—from toilets, showers, kitchen sinks—discharges outside into (ideally) a concrete or glass fiber tank, and is separated into liquids and solids. The liquids (*effluent*) on top float out, through pipes, into a *seepage* pit or into distribution pipes (with holes in the bottom), where these liquids are absorbed into the soil. The solids in the tank are decomposed by bacteria, taking up less space. This buildup of solids should be inspected every two or three years by a disposal company to see whether the solids need to be pumped out. (See Figure 28-1.) The best times for waste removal are late spring or summer, so the bacteria will have several warm months to proliferate once again.

In general, the more rural the community, the more likely that it has septic systems. A summer house is a more likely candidate than a year-round house.

Having your house connected to public sewage lines is far better than having a septic system. You won't have any problems with maintenance, and you don't have to worry so much about what goes down the drain. And you can avoid the worst fate of all: The odor from waste liquids that discharge onto your lawn can take a while to go away.

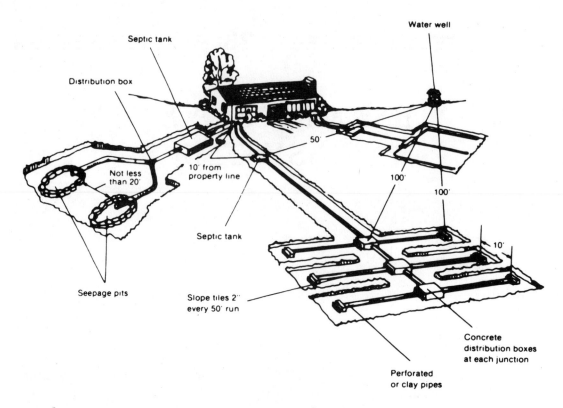

Figure 28-1.   Diagram of septic systems.

A concrete or fiberglass septic tank that's installed and maintained properly should not give you any grief for up to 30 years. Steel tanks may last no more than 10 years.

When questioning sellers or their agents about their private sewer system, ask:

- What type system is it (septic or cesspool)?
- What the septic tank is made of.
- How large the tank is. Generally, you need a 1,000-gallon tank for four people or bedrooms, and 250 gallons more for every other person or bedroom. And don't think that, just because you're thinking of buying a summer house, you need less capacity. Although the system will have the winter months to recover from summer abuse, if you have a big crowd over on one summer weekend, you may have an overflow of not just the crowd.
- How often has it been inspected, when was it last inspected, and when was it last pumped out. (Some homeowners just ignore their systems. They or the subsequent homeowners will eventually pay the price: having a septic system replaced or repaired is expensive.)

- Inquire whether the owners have documents showing the location of the system. If not, check that the system is where they say it is (usually five or ten feet from the house sewer line). You can usually find it by poking an iron pole into the ground. The top of the tank typically is no more than a foot below the surface. Inspectors looking for septic tanks may charge $50 or more an hour. Also, it may be under a lovely new patio, which now has to be ripped up so the tank can be pumped.

- See whether the laundry area or the kitchen has a special sewage line that goes into a dry well (a small underground drainage area, filled with rocks) rather than the septic system, lest grease and soap clog up the drainage field.

- Find out whether a house with a septic system has had new bedrooms added at any time in the past. That would strongly suggest that the system had been built for fewer people than have been living there, perhaps putting a strain on the original septic system.

- Check whether an older house with a septic system has ever had its drainage field replaced, with the liquid diverted to another part of the property. Drainage fields tend to get clogged up over the years if the tank hasn't been pumped out regularly. With a fairly small property, you may have trouble once a few possible drainage fields have become clogged up. There may not be room for another drainage field.

- Check with the municipality whether there have been any septic system problems in this area—perhaps because the soil doesn't readily absorb water or the area has been flooded. Incidentally, if you or the homeseller aren't sure where the tank is situated, town records may give the answer.

- If you're on the verge of buying the house, challenge the system. Flush all toilets three times in succession. Run water into the bathtub for a half an hour or more and watch it drain away. Check that the water goes down quickly. Then visit the lowest drain in the house (the basement shower, for instance, or the laundry sink) to see if the water has backed up as a result of your upstairs tests.

  If the system withstands your water torture, you can almost relax. On the other hand, if water does back up into the laundry sink, it may not mean the end. Perhaps it's simply that the line from the septic tank to the drainage field is blocked. Ask the owner to have the trouble checked. Be there when the workers investigate.

  Then inspect the grounds around the house for effluent or raw sewage. It's not unusual to find effluent from a defective system oozing out of the soil above a drainage field. Even if you don't see escaping sewage, note whether any section of the lawn is much greener than another. (Erma Bombeck was right: The grass really is greener over the septic tank area—if it's not working properly.) Also look for other signs of malfunction, such as ponding in low areas of the drainage field, flies, and odors.

If you do see effluent escaping above the drainage area, you need the advice of an expert. Replacing a drainage field can cost almost as much as building a whole septic system for a new house. One reason: In a yard that's been landscaped, septic system crews have to work carefully, perhaps forgoing the use of heavy equipment. Also, new percolation ("perc") tests will be required, to determine the soil's absorption rate.

- Finally, ask the homeowner how you should treat a septic system. Act dumb. Is there anything little old you shouldn't throw down the toilet? Is there any advice he or she would give you?

  If the owners say you can throw anything you want down the toilet, be worried. They probably have.

Here are the rules:

- Don't throw anything inorganic (that was not once alive) down the system, like cat kitter, sanitary napkins, disposable diapers, painting supplies, or even cigarettes with filters. Installing a garbage disposal system in a house with a septic system is not recommended.

- According to the U.S. Public Health Service, soaps, detergents, bleaches, drain cleaners, and other material normally used in the household can be released into the system—in moderation.

- Fix household leaks promptly, so that they don't saturate your drainage field outside. Leaks in toilets are especially insidious: You may not notice them.

- In winter, be especially careful to conserve water, so that your septic system doesn't develop problems. The ground may be frozen, making repairs and service difficult. Especially in the winter, space out the times you do laundry or wash dishes.

- Take steps at the first sign of trouble: sewage backing up into the house, odors, or dark green grass over the septic tank or drainage field.

- There's disagreement over whether special enzymes can increase the bacterial activity in a tank. The people who favor them tend to be the same people who sell them to homeowners. More impartial observers think that chemical or biological aids or cleaners can interfere with the normal bacterial process. Avoid them.

DOES A HOUSE HAVE A SEPTIC SYSTEM?

Some homesellers don't even know that their houses have septic systems instead of the public sewer lines found in more urban communities.

The owners whom the current homeowners bought from may have obtained permits to connect the house to public sewage lines and even paid the fees. But because their septic system was working, they may have stopped short of paying the several thousand dollars for the actual connection. But they didn't bother telling the new owners, and may even have misled them.

So, if the sellers assure you that their house is connected to a public sewage system, double check. (Even a few houses in cities may have septic systems because the houses were inconveniently far from public sewage lines.)

If you buy such a house, you may not find out about the septic system until the sewage backs up.

Signs that a house now has or once had a septic system:

- The main sewage line is higher than the basement floor instead of level with it.
- The line exits at the rear of a house rather than the front.

If your house definitely has access to public lines now, but had a septic system or cesspool in the past, make sure the old tank or hole has been filled with rocks or soil, to prevent accidents. It's not that unusual for homeowners to suddenly find a big hole on their property, where abandoned septic tanks or cesspools have caved in.

Red Flags

- ✔ Any cesspool.
- ✔ The septic tank is made of steel, which typically lasts only ten years.
- ✔ Too small a tank for your family. (Generally, you need a 1,000-gallon tank for four people and 250 gallons more for every other person.)
- ✔ No evidence that the current tank was pumped out in recent years.
- ✔ No assurance that the owner even knows where the tank is.
- ✔ New bedrooms tacked onto the house after the septic system

was installed. The old system may have been built for fewer residents.

✔ The property is small, and there have been various drainage fields, suggesting that there may not be room for another field.

✔ Common problems in this particular area of town. Check with neighbors.

✔ A backup of water in the lower parts of the house after you flush the toilets and run water down the bathtub.

✔ Signs of problems: ponds on the lawn, odors, flies, greener grass in one area.

✔ The owner didn't treat the system properly and flushed cat litter, sanitary napkins, and other inorganic substances down the toilet.

✔ Evidence that the house has a septic system, even though the owner insists that it's connected to public lines.

29

IS THE HOUSE BURGLAR-RESISTANT?

If there are bars on all the windows of the houses in an area, you're being sent a message: The neighborhood may be unsafe. Talk to the local police and to your prospective neighbors.

With any house at all, you should always determine how crime-proof it is. While houses near major highways are more vulnerable than those in more isolated areas (burglars want quick getaway routes), all residences are at risk. If the owners of a house you admire have done next to nothing to burglar-proof their house, factor in the extra expenses before you buy.

The goal of crime-proofing a residence is to ensure that a burglar spends more than a minute to a minute-and-a-half trying to break in. Beyond that time, according to surveys of convicted burglars, the average criminal becomes very unhappy and thinks seriously about plying his trade elsewhere.

But a house shouldn't be so difficult to break into that it becomes hard for you to escape in a hurry, which you might want to do in an emergency, like a fire.

OUTSIDE THE HOUSE

To check how crime-proof a house is, begin with the outside. Outside lights should be on timers or be set to activate when there is motion or a body is sensed in the immediate area. (See Figure 29-1.) Every possible entrance should be illuminated, especially side doors or back doors not easily visible to neighbors.

Figure 29-1.   Motion-sensitive overhead lighting.

Bushes and shrubbery next to a house should be trimmed. Burglars might slip behind them at dusk, waiting for nightfall to try to break in. They might also use the bushes to conceal an attack on a basement or other lower-level window.

An electronic garage door is more difficult to open than a mechanical one.

A deadbolt lock on a door is one where the bolt doesn't spring back: It's "dead." Burglars armed with a piece of plastic cannot pry back such a bolt, as they might with a spring bolt. A good deadbolt extends at least an inch into the door jamb. It should work on a separate mechanism from a nearby spring lock; otherwise, a burglar can get access to the spring lock and open the deadbolt. All outside doors should have two locks.

For you to get out quickly in case of an emergency, like a fire, dead bolts should not have a key; a mechanical device is better. Obviously, if there is a window panel in the door or adjacent to it, burglars can easily break the glass and flip the lock switch.

A two-cylinder lock must be opened with a key from both outside and inside. Such a lock is better than a one-cylinder model, which allows you to open a door simply by turning the inside knob. If there's a window in the door, burglars could smash it, reach inside, and turn the knob themselves.

For you to see who is ringing your doorbell, a peephole in the door is better than a chain. Door chains give residents a false sense of security; they can easily be broken by a caller.

The best front-door observation system uses an exterior video camera and an interior receiver, so that you can see and talk to any caller before opening the front door, even a bit. For added security, burglar-resistant front doors should not be hollowcore, but be made of metal or solid wood.

Windows that can locked with a key are safer than those that just have latches. If the windows are double-hung (one above the other), the homeowner might drill a hole where they overlap, and then slide a nail or cotter pin into the opening. That way, the window can be locked in an unobstrusive way, giving burglars a hard time figuring out why they can't open it. But be mindful that you yourself might have to leave quickly in an emergency.

A sliding-glass door calls for special protection. Many hardware stores sell locks specifically for such doors. Solid bars that fit into the door's bottom glide channel are effective in deterring access. Higher-quality sliding doors have built-in footlocks.

Basement windows are a nasty business. Although many people put bars over the windows, that's dangerous. What if a child were trapped in the basement during a fire? Another solution: a good lock on the door that links the basement to the rest of the house.

INSIDE THE HOUSE

Determined burglars can enter almost any house, so you need a second line of defense.

If you have valuables to protect, a safe—sunk into concrete in the basement, and concealed—would be desirable.

An alarm system may be worth it, too, if you keep in mind that a good alarm system costs from $1,000 to $2,000 for the average house, and that the average burglar gets away with $1,000 in a break-in.

Police estimate that houses with alarms are burglarized only one-third to one-sixth as often as houses without them.

For $300 to $400 you can get the minimal protection, suitable for an apartment—electronic protection on two doors, with a motion detector that covers a few rooms. The motion detector can be programmed to overlook anything near a floor, like pets. Protecting an average-sized house would cost $1,000 and up.

Alarms can be local, emitting a noise to alert the neighbors. That may or may not be effective. In a quiet, suburban neighborhood, where the neighbors are friendly, an alarm may help. In a noisy neighborhood, forget it.

Alarms may also be connected to a central control system, where security people remain day and night waiting for the devices to give signals. The monthly cost is around $25. In a sophisticated system, the control station people can detect whether the alarm is from a fire or a burglary and, if a burglary, where the entry came. The control station people will normally phone the house first to verify that it's not a false alarm.

BURGLARY PREVENTION CHECKLIST

Doors

- ☐ Are all outside doors of metal or solid wood?
- ☐ Are door frames strong enough and tight enough to prevent forcing or spreading?
- ☐ Are door hinges protected from removal from the outside?
- ☐ Are there no windows in any door—or at least none within 40 inches of the locks?
- ☐ Are all door locks adequate and in good repair?
- ☐ Are strikes and strike plates adequate and properly installed?
- ☐ Is the locking mechanism out of reach through a mail slot, delivery port, or pet entrance at the doorway?
- ☐ Is there a screen or storm door with an adequate lock?
- ☐ Are all entrances lighted with at least a 40-watt light?
- ☐ Can the front entrance be observed by someone in the street or other public area?
- ☐ Does the porch or landscaping offer someone concealment from view from street or public area?
- ☐ If there is a glass sliding door, is the sliding panel secured from being lifted out of the track?
- ☐ Is a Charlie-bar or key-operated auxiliary lock used on sliding glass doors?
- ☐ Do you have a name plate on your mailbox or door? Knowing your name can enable an intruder to pretend he or she knows you.

Garage and Basement

- ☐ Are all entrances to living quarters from garage and basement made of metal or solid wood?
- ☐ Does the door from garage to living quarters have adequate locks?

Windows

☐ Do all windows have adequate locks in operating condition?

☐ Do windows have screens or storm windows that lock from the inside?

☐ Do no windows offer invitations to burglars?

☐ Do windows that open to unprotected areas have secure screens or grilles?

☐ Are exterior areas of windows free from any structures or landscaping that might conceal them?

☐ Is the exterior adequately lit at all window areas?

☐ Are trees and shrubbery kept trimmed back from upper floor windows?

☐ Are ladders not kept outside the house, where they may be accessible?

Basement Doors and Windows

☐ Is there no door from the outside to the basement?

☐ If there is, is that door adequately secured?

☐ Is the outside basement entrance lit by a light of at least 40 watts?

☐ Can the outside basement door be seen from the street or by neighbors?

☐ Are all basement windows adequately secured?

Garage Doors and Windows

☐ Is the outside entrance door to the garage equipped with an adequate locking device?

☐ Are garage windows secured adequately for ground-floor windows?

☐ Are tools and ladders kept in the garage and not outside?

☐ Are all garage doors lit on the outside by at least a 40-watt light?

☐ Can you deactivate the garage door opener when on vacation?

Source: The National Sheriffs' Association.

30

TERMITES
AND OTHER INSECTS

Ask homeowners what scares them the most, and they may not talk about radon, climbing property taxes, the baby bust's effect on house prices, electromagnetic radiation, or the possibility that the wonderful tax breaks that homeowners receive might be repealed. Their answer may be termites and carpenter ants.

Folklore has it that carpenter ants do even more damage than termites—and termites, to quote the literature of the National Pest Control Association (NPCA) in Dunn Loring, Virginia, "do more damage than fires, storms, and earthquakes combined."

Actually, termites are far worse than carpenter ants, which are mainly just nuisances. And fires are far more destructive than termites. The NPCA's researcher, George Rambo, estimates that termites cause $750 million worth of property damage in this country every year. The Insurance Information Institute estimates that fires did $9.262 billion worth of damage in 1988, not including destruction of government property and forests. That's 12.35 times as much.

MEET THE TERMITE

There's no reason for a homebuyer to automatically reject any house that has termites. The common estimate is that 25 percent of all residences in areas like the South and the Northeast have or have had termites. The incidence may be as high as 40 percent, and 50 percent in areas where houses are 50 or 60 years old.

Homebuyers shouldn't panic even if there's evidence of termite activity in any residence they check. Termites destroy wood very slowly, over several years. (See Figure 30-1.)

Another reason not to panic is that all sorts of new tools are available to detect termites, like fiber-optic devices that let inspectors peer into small openings, and even dogs trained to sniff out termites by the gases they emit. Dogs, in the view of some experts, are close to being 100-percent effective.

Dogs are especially good at finding termites in houses with slab foundations, where inspectors cannot check basements or crawl spaces for infestation. The animals, which announce the presence of termites by scratching on the wood, can sometimes find termites where you would not expect the darling little critters—like oceanliners.

Figure 30-1.   Termite damage.

MEET THE CARPENTER ANT

Although carpenter ants damage wood by gnawing out space for their nests, the wood usually has been damaged by moisture already. The main reason termites do so much more damage is that termites actually eat the wood. Carpenter ants usually don't do measurable damage.

Unlike termites, carpenter ants are easy to spot. If you don't see them in person, you may spot the wood dust they expel after they tunnel into wood.

CAUSE FOR WORRY

Wood-destroying insects shouldn't send you to an early grave, but you should certainly be concerned. While termites do their damage slowly, they're tireless. They work 24 hours a day, 365 days a year. Given enough time, they can, not surprisingly, eat you out of house and home. Some houses, ravaged by termites over 10 or 15 years, have had to be abandoned and torn down.

Insurance policies don't compensate homeowners for destruction caused by termites. Also, because the damage is slow, it's not considered a tax-deductible casualty loss, although in a few weird cases tax courts have been persuaded that certain homeowners were the victims of "fast" termites.

Don't feel invulnerable if you happen to live in a brick house. Termites can go after the wood in the window frame, the wood girders, the wood joists, and the wall framing. Also, don't think you're safe if your house is new. A new house can become infested with termites even before construction is completed.

Don't think you're home-free if your house has termite shields (barriers between the foundation and the frame). A shield may have been made of tarpaper and not metal, or it may not have been thick enough. Also, termites may have been able to penetrate the seams, or build mud tunnels around them. As for the pressure-treated wood that has replaced shields in recent year, exterminators have seen termites bypass treated wood.

Don't relax even if termaticides were sprayed around the foundation or into the ground below your house a few years ago. Since then, the chemicals may have lost their effectiveness. Pest control people still yearn for the days when the long-lasting chemical chlordane could be used against termites. The government banned its use in 1988 because of questions about its safety. "Nothing is even almost as good as chlordane," says Douglas Mampe, a world-famous entomologist.

The bad news about carpenter ants is that any quarter-inch or larger black ant you see in your house probably is one. And although they're easier to identify than termites, these ants are more trouble to eradicate: Finding their nests is hard because they don't build tunnels, they don't remain in only one place, and an entire colony can move to new quarters fast. When exterminators bid on a job to eliminate carpenter ants, they figure that half the time they will have to make two visits and treatments to eliminate a serious infestation.

Carpenter ants are migratory; they often drop into houses from nearby trees. Chances are high that you will eventually experience carpenter ants if you purchase a house in the country or on a heavily wooded lot.

FINDING AN EXTERMINATOR

If you're buying a house that has termites as tenants, in your search for an exterminator get several bids. Simple termite treatment may cost $400 to $800, but can go as high as $1,200 to $1,400 or even more if carpentry repair is needed. Treating carpenter ants costs from $100 to $700, with $200 to $300 being typical. Check whether you're getting a guarantee, and for how long (a year is typical).

Find out exactly what the pest control company will do and why. If the problem is carpenter ants, does the exterminator think that the nest is outside the home or inside? If outside, he or she should apply insecticide around the exterior; if inside, he or she should inject insecticide into openings ("voids") where they may be living. Ant traps are usually not highly effective, one reason being that ants will randomly search for food, not eat just poisoned food put in one place.

Besides price, check how long a company has been in business. A "lifetime guarantee" isn't worth much if the company won't be around next year. Mampe suggests favoring a company that has been in business for 10 to 20 years. Also give credit to a company that belongs to the NPCA, which keeps its members current on new technology and provides you with a place to lodge a complaint if you have one.

You can call in an exterminator any time of the year, but Mampe recommends that you avoid having insecticide sprayed outside when the ground is frozen or when the soil is very wet. The chemicals become diluted and may spread to areas where you don't want them.

SIGNS OF TERMITES

- Seeing swarms in a house in the spring or fall;
- Spotting discarded wings (on window sills, for example);

- Noticing mud tunnels that the insects use to travel from the earth to the wood that they eat (see Figure 30-2); and
- Discovering wood that's been eaten away on the inside.

KEEPING TERMITES AND CARPENTER ANTS AT BAY

If you're checking a house for termites, look for these warning signs:

- Scrap lumber or firewood is stored near the house.
- A house's wood siding, floor joists, and wall studs are in contact with the ground. Latticework under a porch is touching the soil. (The outside soil should be at least six inches below all woodwork.)

Also be certain that all rainwater drains away from a house, perhaps by means of drainage tiles installed around the outside of foundation footings and that gutters and leaders are working properly. Check that all windows, but especially basement windows, are made of chemically treated wood or metal. The window wells should be free of leaves and trash, and have drainage for rainwater.

To ward off carpenter ants, fix any moisture problems you may have. Water may cause wood to decay, and the rotting wood may

Figure 30-2.   Termite tube on interior wall.

attract ants. Check for leaks in the roof, around windows, around chimneys and skylights, around plumbing fixtures, and around sump pumps. Look for clogged drain gutters. See that your air conditioners are draining properly. You might spray insecticide into any cracks or openings you see, and plug them up. Carpenter ants have a sweet tooth, so keep food areas clean.

Inspect your house every month or so for insect infestation (every few weeks in warm-weather months).

WHERE TERMITES CAN ENTER

- Door jambs (subject to exposure from the outside environment, and often abut porches, patios, decks, and even soil);
- Expansion joints;
- Cracks around plumbing or electrical pipes;
- Cracks in the foundation slab;

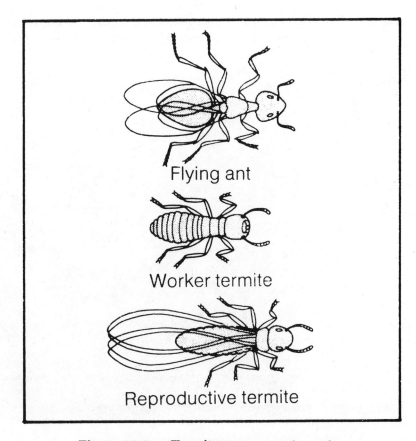

Figure 30-3.   Termites vs. carpenter ants.

- Concrete slabs, with minute cracks that can allow termites to enter;
- Crawl spaces that allow termites to build their mud tubes along the foundation wall and support piers; and
- Garage door framing.

TERMITES VS. ANTS

It's easy to confuse flying termites and flying ants: They basically look alike. (Flying ants may or may not be carpenter ants.) The differences include:

- Ants have pinched waists.
- The abdomens of ants are separated from their bodies by thin stems. With termites, the abdomens are joined to the bodies without any stems.
- Ants have two sets of wings of different sizes, while termite wings are about the same size.
- Both ants and termites tend to shed their wings after swarming to new areas. If you place the wings on dark paper, you will

Figure 30-4.   Wooden deck touching ground.

see that ant wings have a few prominent dark veins; termite wings have thin veins that are the same color as the wings.

- Termite antennae are almost straight. If you inspect them with a magnifying glass, they look like a string of beads. Ant antennae are shaped like elbows.
- Their size can give you a clue. Ants range from one-eighth to three-quarters of an inch. Termites are three-eighths of an inch. (See Figure 30-3.)

Red Flags

✔ Invitations for termites (wood from the house in contact with the ground, scrap lumber or firewood stored near the house).

✔ Termites clearly present (swarms in the spring or fall, discarded wings in the house, mud tunnels inside or outside the house).

✔ Termites have already done considerable damage: A good deal of wood has been eaten away on the inside.

✔ Trees that overhang the house—an entry route for carpenter ants.

✔ Any wood areas continuously exposed to moisure, like flat roof framing. (See Figure 30-4.)

✔ Areas where wood is continually exposed to moisture.

THE WORST HOME IMPROVEMENT MISTAKES

Once you buy a house, you may decide to spring for various home improvements, just to turn the place into your true dream house.

Just be wary.

Here are some examples of home-improvement mistakes:

- One homeowner figured something was amiss when, one cold morning, the toilet bowl in his new bathroom began steaming. The contractor, it turned out, had connected the toilet to a hot-water pipe.

- Another homeowner, in a $500,000 house, had recently paid to have a new bathroom installed on the second floor. He took a leisurely shower, let the water drain, and went downstairs. The bathroom floor collapsed. The contractor had neglected to connect the bathtub drain to the drainpipe, and all the water had simply poured into the floor.

- In another case, a contractor installed a new recreation room onto a house but was careless about the footings, not planting them in undisturbed soil. The rec room settled and broke off from the house, creating a gap as wide as six inches in places.

Horror stories about home improvements abound because homeowners continue to make the same old mistakes. Why don't they learn? Among the reasons:

- They don't spring for improvements that often, so they don't learn by heart the steps they should follow—finding the names of contractors, asking them for references, interviewing those references, making sure the contract specifies such things as how often any debris is carted off, and so forth.

- People get seduced by the opportunity of seemingly saving a lot of money by accepting a very low bid, without realizing that there are always some contractors out there on the brink of financial ruin. These contractors will promise anything to get a job—for example, swear that they will renovate your bathroom for a pittance, even if they have never installed a faucet in their lives. Once they have worked a while, they may insist that the bid was an underestimate and demand a lot more money, or they'll walk away, leaving the job barely begun. (Other contractors usually hate taking over unfinished jobs: They don't know how badly done any concealed work might have been.)

- Expecting your money back—Most home improvements don't fully justify your investment, unless they solve serious problems (for example, your kitchen belongs in the Addams family house).

- Not agreeing on terms and specifications—A fellow in Arlington, Virginia, agreed to pay $100,000 for a remodeling job that would have doubled the size of house. Soon after, he asked the contractor when the new kitchen cabinets would arrive. At that point the contractor announced that "new cabinets will be $5,000 to $10,000 extra."

- Accepting the lowest bid—The story is told of the astronaut who became panicky just before being shot into space. There he was, atop 14 stories of equipment, when the thought entered his head: "Everything below me was built by the lowest bidder."

  A low bid may mean bad materials and good workers, good materials and bad workers, or—worst of all—bad materials and bad workers.

- Asking for the impossible—Expecting a good quality carpet for $14 a square yard, for example.

- Not putting changes in writing—Unless you insert a change into a contract, you may not get what you had hoped for, warns Brian Patchan, executive director of the National Remodeling Council. "If the contract called for sliding-glass doors, you may decide that you want French doors, with small-pane glass, instead," he notes. "But unless you put it in writing, you may wind up with ordinary doors."

- Getting reliable names—Run any contractors' names you have past a chapter of the local Better Business Bureau. Look for a pattern of complaints, not occasional complaints. Also make sure that any candidates belong to the National Association of the Remodeling Industry in Arlington, or the National Remodeling Council of the National Association of Home Builders in Washington, D.C.

- Not checking references—What you want are no nasty surprises. That's why you should ask a contractor for the names of people that he or she has recently done work for. Ask those customers: Did the contractor come close to his time targets and estimates? Did he or she clean up after himself? Did he or she disappear mysteriously for weeks at a time (to work on another project)? Would you hire him or her again, without hesitation?

- Paying too quickly—The golden rule is to pay contractors slow. Pay any contractor for a quarter of a project when a quarter of the work is completed, half when half is completed, and so on.

- Not reading the contract—A good contract describes how debris will be cleaned up and how often (ideally, every night); how house furnishings will be protected; when the work will begin and when it will end; what happens if you cancel the contract; and what defenses you have against property liens that any plumbers, electricians, and other subcontractors might lodge against you if the remodeler fails to pay them.

- Not considering a lawyer—Think of hiring one if the expense is high (over $5,000) or if the work involves safety, such as your having asbestos removed. A clever lawyer, for instance, might insert a clause assessing a financial penalty if the remodeler starts work late or finishes late.

- Not considering an architect—The conventional wisdom is that you should hire an architect if a project is structural (it involves weight-bearing walls and ceilings) and if the front of your house will be altered (an unattractive front can drastically lower your property's value). But architects can accomplish more: Arrange for a spirited bidding competition, make sure the contractors are bidding on the same things, and check that any contractor really uses the top-grade materials he or she promised to use.

- Falling into "the Taj Mahal trap"—Don't overimprove your house for the neighborhood. To put it another way, if yours is an ordinary house in an ordinary neighborhood, don't install $30,000 black-walnut cabinets in your kitchen.

- Being self-indulgent—Don't install a darkroom for photography, or build a six-car garage for your antique cars, unless you're willing to have them removed when you sell. Real estate agents have a term for houses that have been improved so self-indulgently that the market for them has shrunk into near-invisibility: one-owner houses.

- Not checking a contractor's insurance—Professional remodelers carry the complete range of liability insurance that protects them and you in case of personal injury on the job, damage to your house, and so on.

WHAT YOU WILL RECOUP?

Many homeowners wrongly assume that improvements will pay for themselves when the house is sold. Actually, few remodeling jobs return 100 cents on the dollar. Those that return the most are new or remodeled bathrooms, new or remodeled kitchens, and family room additions. But the returns can vary from community to community, as shown by this chart comparing returns in Ridgewood, New Jersey (R), and Princeton, New Jersey (P), two upscale towns. Local real estate agents estimated how much of the costs were recovered. Source: *Remodeling* Magazine.

Family Room Addition

Project: Add a 16-by-25–foot, light-filled room on a new crawl space foundation with wood-joist floor framing, matching wood siding on exterior walls, and matching fiberglass shingle roof. Include drywall interior with insulation; 120 square feet of glass (doors and windows).

Advice: In demand are fireplaces, skylights, a cathedral ceiling, built-in cabinets, and bookshelves.

	Cost	Resale Value	Cost Recouped
(R)	$36,016	$34,019	94%
(P)	$33,471	$26,736	80%

Major Kitchen Remodeling

Project: Update 170-square-foot kitchen, with design and installation of 30 feet of new mid-priced cabinets, laminated countertops, a 3 x 5 foot island, an energy-efficient oven, a cook top with ventilation system, a microwave, a dishwasher, a garbage disposal, and custom lighting. Also, new resilient floor, wall coverings, and ceiling treatments.

Advice: A light, white kitchen is best, preferably opening onto a family room. Needed is an efficient work triangle and lots of storage space. Polyurethane-treated hardwood floors are popular. Also in demand are pantries, undercabinet lighting, and big storage drawers.

	Cost	Resale Value	Cost Recouped
(R)	$22,863	$21,167	93%
(P)	$22,454	$16,227	72%

Bath Addition

Project: Add a second full bath, 6 feet by 8 feet, within existing floor plan, to a one- or one-and-a-half–bath house. Include cultured-marble vanity top, molded sink, standard bathtub with shower, low-profile toilet, lighting, mirrored medicine cabinet, linen storage, vinyl wallpaper, and ceramic-tile floor and walls in tub area.

Advice: Should be inconspicuously placed off a hallway, near bedrooms or family room. Cabinets and good lighting (especially skylights) are recommended.

	Cost	Resale Value	Cost Recouped
(R)	$12,307	$12,769	104%
(P)	$12,175	$11,710	96%

Siding Replacement

Project: Install 2,000 square feet of vinyl or aluminum siding using quarter-inch insulating foam board. Include new soffits, fascia and trim, and gutters.

Advice: Wood siding will return more than vinyl or aluminum.

	Cost	Resale Value	Cost Recouped
(R)	$9,522	$6,007	63%
(P)	$8,859	$5,908	67%

Bath Remodeling

Project: Install new standard-size tub, commode, and solid surface vanity counter with molded sinks in a 5-by-9–foot bathroom. Also install new lighting, mirrored medicine cabinet, and ceramic tile floor and walls in tub/shower area (vinyl wallpaper elsewhere).

Advice: Pedestal lavatories and big mirrors give small rooms a sense of space. Skylights can brighten dark rooms. Consider his-and-her sinks.

	Cost	Resale Value	Cost Recouped
(R)	$8,592	$5,967	69%
(P)	$8,401	$6,601	79%

Window Replacement

Project: Replace 16 single-pane windows with energy-efficient vinyl or vinyl-clad aluminum double-pane windows.

Advice: Wood-frame windows are especially popular in the Northeast, with its more traditional architecture.

	Cost	Resale Value	Cost Recouped
(R)	$7,562	$4,833	64%
(P)	$7,270	$5,227	72%

Deck Addition

Project: Add a 16-by-20–foot deck of pressure-treated pine. Include a built-in bench, railings, and planter, also of pressure-treated pine.

Advice: Ideally, decks should be off the family room or master bedroom. Multi-level decks are in demand. Design interest can be raised with diagonal boards, or by the addition of a bench or planter box.

	Cost	Resale Value	Cost Recouped
(R)	$6,771	$3,667	54%
(P)	$6,090	$4,632	76%

Appendix 2

ROUTINE HOME MAINTENANCE

These days, more and more homeowners are treating their houses like motels: as places just to eat, watch TV, and sleep.

Some people almost never visit their own basements or attics, and wouldn't notice a roof leak until the water made its way through the attic floor to the bedroom ceiling.

Folks have neglected their houses for the very same reason we have so many latchkey children: Both parents are working. Mom and Dad are now simply too busy and too tired to maintain their houses properly. The problem is compounded with single heads of household.

Another reason so many houses are neglected is that it's become more difficult to get repairpeople to do minor jobs. They may give you an estimate, but you may never hear from them again. They want to do big, expensive jobs, not routine, low-cost repairs. The operative word among contracters today is "replace," not "repair."

But if any homeowner neglects the small, inexpensive repairs, they can balloon into big, costly emergency repairs. Loose shower tiles, for example, may let water destroy the tile support boards and seep behind the metal pan below the floor, damaging the ceiling of the room below. A furnace or air conditioner that's never inspected or maintained may last only half as long as well-maintained units. A furnace that's never serviced may last only 10 years, not 15 or 20.

The best advice is to tour your entire house periodically, looking for leaks, rust, corrosion, loose tiles, cracks—anything out of the ordinary. Learn the life expectancies of the various elements of the house, so you'll gain a better idea of when to pay for repairs and when to pay for replacements. Also, bear in mind that the best time to have any work done is just before something stops working altogether.

Here's a quick guide to routine home maintenance:

Furnaces/Boilers—With a hot-air system, remove the front panel and, while the system is on, check the flame at the burners. If it's blue, it's working well. But if there are white cones on top or the flame is dancing, you may have trouble. You may have a crack in the heat exchanger, or the gases may not be drawn to the chimney.

Change the air filter every month (filters are either washable or disposable). Be sure to insert the new filter in the proper "flow" direction.

With a hot-water furnace, be sure to oil the pump(s) that pulls the water through the system. Use a clear lubricating oil in the three openings four or five times a season. You may add five years to the life of the pump(s).

Regularly check the pressure gauge that every hot-water boiler has. If the reading is above 20 psi, something is amiss. (See Figure A2-1.)

Figure A2-1.   Boiler pressure-temperature gauge.

Steam boilers tend to be old and therefore require more attention than other systems. Check that the sight glass, which indicates the water level, is half to three-quarters full. If it's more, steam may come out of the relief valves. Make sure the water is clean, not rusty. Every three or four weeks, remove several buckets of water to get rid of dirt and minerals, which could clog the relief valves. Let fresh water in gradually. (Newer systems have an automatic feed, so the new water comes in slowly.)

Hot-Water Heaters—If you follow the manufacturer's directions, you will faithfully drain the heater every few months to remove mineral or rust buildup at the bottom of the tank. The problem is that most homeowners do not follow this procedure, and when they infrequently attempt to draw water from the drain, they have trouble reseating the drain. This results in an ongoing leak and much frustration. The best advice is to leave the heater alone if you've ignored it for a number of years. Watch for signs of rusting or leaking and listen for popping sounds; these are the precursors to tank failure. Replace a hot water heater before it fails. If it bursts, 50 gallons of hot water can do a lot of damage.

Bathrooms—Check all the fixtures for signs of water seepage (cracked or missing caulking or grout). Tap all bathtub and shower stall tile work for soundness. Repair any leaks or dripping—your utility dollars may be literally going down the drain.

Basements—Look for damp spots. Water may be coming in from below or from the walls. The simplest solution is to make sure that the leaders, which capture rainwater from the roof, are discharging the water away from the house, and that the soil around the house is graded away from the foundation, so that water flows away from and not toward the house.

If these steps don't work, consider a sump pump, which will automatically pump basement water to the outside. Be certain the water is discharged away from the foundation or you will indeed have circulating water. If the water in your basement is so deep that it's measured in inches, a French drain may be the answer. Such a drain is installed under the floor of the basement to draw water outside.

Also, check the basement walls regularly. A vertical crack may simply mean the foundation is settling. You can caulk such a crack. That could also reduce any radon infiltration.

A horizontal crack, on the other hand, may mean that outside dirt or water is pushing the wall inward. You may even see a bulge. Call in an engineer for analysis.

Roofs—If an asphalt roof is 20 years old or older and the shingles are dry and curling, start getting worried.

Leaks are usually caused by pinholes and cracking in the

flashings of a roof, especially around the chimney, where the tar or caulk may be alternately heated and cooled by the elements. If your roof is only 10 years old and in good shape, don't be talked into having it replaced. Just have the flashings tarred or caulked, as necessary. Over 90 percent of roof leaks are caused by faulty flashings and not by worn roofing materials.

Shade trees around your house can extend the life of your roof. So can venting your attic properly, so that moisture can escape and not damage insulation, and heat can escape and not dry the roof.

Use binoculars to inspect the roof for broken or missing shingles and for curling. Check the sunny side of a house, which may have the worst damage. If you're having a roof replaced, do it during the summer, if possible, when the shingles are more pliable.

Kitchen Appliances—Make sure that the seals on all your appliances (refrigerator, dishwasher, oven) are tight. With a refrigerator, vacuum the condenser coils at the rear several times a year to increase their efficiency. Some automatic-defrosting refrigerators have pans underneath to trap water. Check the buildup every once in a while, lest mold or fungus appear. Check the operation of ice-makers—often a troublemaker as well.

With a gas oven, be sure the flame is blue. If the flame is white or yellow, it should be adjusted. Make sure the thermostat is accurate. Put a metal thermometer into the oven to see that it reaches the specified temperature. If there's a discrepancy, adjust the thermostat dial.

With a dishwasher, regularly examine the bottom of the door— the most vulnerable area—for corrosion. When the cycle is through, see that only a little water is left in the machine, at the bottom of the pump intake area. Every so often, pull the bottom panel off to make sure that the machinery hasn't been damaged by leakage. Check the area around the dishwasher for any signs of water leakage (stains, floor damage).

WHEN A HOUSE WEARS OUT

	Expected Life Span (Years)	Cost to Replace ($)
Roof		
Wood shingles	15–25	2,000–3,000
Asphalt shingles	15–20	1,500–2,200
Cedar shakes	20–40	3,000–5,000
Kitchen Appliances	8–15	500–1,000 each

	Expected Life Span (Years)	Cost to Replace ($)
Gutters/Downspouts	20–30	600–900
Central Air Conditioning		
Compressor	6–10	800–1,000
Compressor/ condenser	10–20	1,500–2,000
Heating		
Hot-air furnace	15–20	1,500–1,800
Hot-water boiler	20–25	2,000–2,500
Water heater	7–12	350–500

Appendix 3

UNAPPROVED IMPROVEMENTS

Something even a home inspector cannot do for you is tell whether the third bedroom, the deck, the new roof, or whatever in the house you're thinking of buying satisfies the local building code, and whether or not the seller ever obtained a building permit for the improvement and, later on, paid the property taxes that he or she should have.

A good many homeowners ignore the rules and pay the penalties, because the improvements they spring for may be unsafe or because they may be fined by the local building department for ignoring the rules. The buyers of those houses may suffer later on.

A few years ago, in Wayne, New Jersey, a man was adding an extra bedroom to his house without a permit. After a heavy snowstorm, the roof of the bedroom collapsed, killing his child.

Other homeowners have been forced to turn their garages (for example) back into garages after turning them into offices or spare bedrooms without proper permits and approvals. One family's house burned down because of a new, defective fireplace. When the owner learned that the former owner had never obtained a building permit for the fireplace, he sued and won.

Many homeowners don't obtain permits simply because they are unaware of the rules. Or they may arrogantly believe that "It's my home, and I can do with it what I want." Or they may just want to avoid having their property taxes increase. (See Figure A3-1.)

How common illegal improvements are seems to depend on the community—whether the inspectors are zealous about checking for additions, whether citizens are aware of the rules, whether the

Figure A3-1.   Building permit sticker.

community is so small and contained that building activity cannot easily go undetected.

New decks are among the most frequent violations, but they are rivaled by new kitchens, new bathrooms, and refinished basements.

A homeowner doesn't need a permit to make ordinary repairs, such as replacing a light fixture or an oven. But the rules can be surprising.

You don't normally need a permit to install a driveway or a sidewalk. But you may need one to install windows of sizes different from the ones before. If you install five new light fixtures or replace an electric oven with a gas oven, check whether you need a permit.

A building permit's cost may be as little as $10 or as much as $1,000, depending on what you spend for the improvement, its size, and the community. The typical cost is $100 to $300. After obtaining a permit, homeowners must be sure that any improvements comply with local and state construction codes.

Contractors are more careful than homeowners about obtaining permits and arranging for inspections, apparently because they have more to lose if they get caught. Still, homeowners should verify that their contractors have obtained the necessary documents and have not just pocketed the money they obtained from the homeowners for the permits. Permits should be posted in public view.

Penalties for infractions can be as high as $500 a day per violation per "discipline" (electrical, plumbing, fire, building). That could mean $2,000 a day. But construction officials tend to take it easy on errant homeowers, and may just warn them to get a permit within 30 days. But there's little mercy if the offender is a contractor—or a homeowner who has previously been warned.

A local building department routinely notifies the local tax assessor about improvements, so that a property's taxes can be raised. But if the assessor learns about an improvement that was made years before, he or she probably cannot collect taxes for those missing years. The reason is that the assessor cannot readily determine when the improvement was made. An assessor can boost taxes only for the next year, or for the current year if he or she files an appeal with the county board of taxation.

FINDING VIOLATIONS

In some communities, inspectors regularly drive around looking for signs of building activity (lumber stacked next to a house, contractors' trucks, building debris, a discarded hot-water heater). Even if they just hear the sound of hammering or sawing, they may stop to inquire. Sometimes residents telephone the building department to complain: "I had to get a permit—why doesn't my neighbor?"

Certain communities require that homeowners selling or renting their houses have them inspected for safety and obtain a "certificate of continued occupancy" or a "certificate of habitability." While the inspectors are checking that the houses have smoke detectors and that the pools are surrounded by fences that comply with local laws, they're also looking for illegal additions.

When someone buys a house, the contract will state that the house complies with local laws. The seller may also sign an affidavit to that effect. But buyers or their lawyers should check the building department's file on the house, to make sure that any major additions, like a swimming pool, were approved.

A QUESTION OF SAFETY

Homeowners who don't obtain permits, hoping to save on property taxes, are putting money ahead of safety.

Turning a basement into a bedroom can be hazardous if there's no second exit in case of an emergency. Changes to plumbing can cause illness if waste water pipes are confused with drinking-water pipes. Structural errors can cause buildings to collapse. Defects in furnaces and in electrical systems can cause fires.

Even decks can be dangerous if built improperly. One construction official recalls a deck, built high off the ground, that collapsed a few years ago, sending 15 people to a hospital.

When You Need a Permit

The state you live in determines whether you need a permit from your town's building department before you spring for particular improvements. But, by and large, permits are needed for:

- Installing new siding;
- Replacing a roof;
- Constructing a deck;
- Installing a dishwasher;
- Adding a bedroom or bathroom;
- Replacing an electric stove with a gas stove;
- Changing plumbing fixtures; and
- Finishing a basement.

When You Don't Need a Permit

You don't normally need a permit for ordinary repairs on a one- or two-story dwelling. Such repairs include:

- Repairing roof material with like material, if the area doesn't exceed 25 percent of the roof within one year;
- Painting the exterior or interior;
- Covering walls, plastering, or placing a drywall on an existing wall;
- Replacing any faucet or valve, if the piping system doesn't have to be rearranged;
- Repairing and replacing duct work;
- Installing floor material, including carpeting;
- Replacing any window or door, if no change in the dimensions or framing of the opening is involved; and
- Replacing glass in any window or door, if the replacement glass conforms to minimum requirements.

═══ Appendix 4 ═══

CHOOSING A REAL ESTATE AGENT

The agent you don't want to list your house with is someone like Lois Flagston—she of the comic strip, "Hi and Lois." Her family is forever teasing her because she never succeeds in selling any houses. Why? The cartoonist who creates "Hi and Lois" knows the answer. She works only part-time. (He also points out that Lois sometimes *does* sell houses. Such contradictions, he explains, are permitted in comic strips.)

Part-time agents should be anathema. Such an agent may be a neighbor, your sister or brother-in-law, or your boss's niece. Such an agent may be as charming as Lois Flagston. Even so, think of an innocuous excuse ("I promised to list my house with my spouse's mother's firm"), and choose someone more appropriate.

The trouble with part-timers is that they may have trouble staying on top of the market. If you're a buyer, they may not show you the creampuff of a house that just came onto the market. If you're a seller, they may not quickly bring around the buyers who just have been transferred from Timbuktu—and tomorrow may be too late. Part-timers may not be in the office to argue for more advertising for their listed houses or to hear a presentation from a local mortgage company. They just may not be there to nourish and nurture a listing.

What about a fine agent who, unfortunately, works for a mediocre firm? In general, pay more attention to the agent than to the firm. But given a choice between two agents, one who works for a good firm and one whose firm has a reputation for stinginess, laziness, nastiness, and incompetence, choose the former.

The choice of agent matters less in a seller's market. Almost every house will sell quickly. But in an ordinary market or in a buyer's market, your choice may mean the difference between your selling your house fast, at a good price, and your selling your house slowly (if at all) for a lower price. Bear in mind that just 10 percent of all agents account for the great majority of house sales. They are the faces you see again and again at awards ceremonies for members of the Million Dollar Club (agents who sell many houses).

Don't understimate the amount of help that agents can give you. They have lots of work to do. Their jobs include:

- Helping you set a price for your house;
- Suggesting ways to improve its appeal;
- Marketing the home through ads, mailings, open houses, circulars, fact sheets, and so forth;
- Telling you what potential buyers think of your house and whether you should make changes;
- Screening buyers to make sure that they can afford your house and are serious about buying it;
- Passing along all offers; and
- Being a catalyst at the closing, where the ownership changes hands.

What else distinguishes members of the Million Dollar Club from agents like Lois Flagston? Carry-through, says one agent. When the top 10 percent tell you in the morning that they'll report to you in the afternoon, they report in the afternoon, not the next day. They're also well-organized. They know at 9 A.M. what they will be doing at noontime and what they will be doing at 4:30 P.M.

They pay attention to detail. Many a sale falls through because the agent neglected important details, such as inquiring whether there has been a dispute over the homeowner's property lines or whether the heating bill was really what the homeowner claimed. A detail-minded agent will also ask you vital questions, such as whether your house is insulated, whether there have been any property disputes, whether the roof or basement have ever leaked, whether the septic system has ever overflowed, whether you have ever had termites, and so forth.

Another trouble with Lois Flagston is that she doesn't take real estate seriously enough to obtain advanced certifications, such as becoming a graduate of the Realty Institute, or a Certified Residential Specialist.

Certainly favor a broker who's a member of the National Association of Realtors. Such a broker will have access to educational materials, and must abide by a special code of ethics. And if you ever have a complaint against an agent, you will know where to complain.

The size of the agency matters less than the ratio of managers to salespeople. There should be one manager for every seven or eight salespeople. Otherwise, the salespeople may have no one to cover for them, and they may not have help in making difficult decisions, such as suggesting that sellers accept or reject a particular offer.

Finally, visit the agency. Questions to ask yourself include: Are there many cars out front? Does the staff work at night and on weekends? Are the agents actually working, or are they chatting around the coffee machine? Is the office and staff presentable and professional?

If you're a seller, have two or three agents from different firms come to your house to give you market analyses and explain their marketing plan to you. Ask them how many houses they have sold in the past year. Ask who covers for the agent when he or she is unavailable. Ask how their firm's approach is better than their competitors' approaches.

If you're a buyer, ask other buyers which agents and brokerage firms they used and how satisfied they were. Was there regular communication? Were there regular house showings? Did their agents keep them informed of new listings? Also if you're a buyer, don't just stop at an agency and get assigned whoever happens to be free. Says one manager, "If someone drops in, I may just assign him an agent who's been going through a dry spell." In other words, Lois Flagston.

AGENTS, BROKERS, REALTORS

Agents can be either brokers or salespeople, but the word "agent" usually means a salesperson.

A salesperson passes a less difficult test than the one a broker must pass, and needs no experience at all. Unlike brokers, salespeople cannot open their own offices. *Salespeople* must work for *brokers*. A Realtor is a broker who is a member of the National Association of Realtors. (Salespeople can become Associate Realtors.)

Keep in mind that most agents work for the seller, and are morally and legally obligated to obtain the best possible price and the best possible terms for the seller, not for the buyer.

A buyer's broker (more properly, buyer's agent) is a person hired by a buyer. Buyer's brokers are becoming more common.

Checklist for Finding the Right Agent

☐   Is the agent full-time?
☐   Is he or she detail-oriented?

- ☐ Is he or she full of energy and enthusiasm? (You don't want someone who gets discouraged easily.)
- ☐ Is he or she experienced?
- ☐ Is he or she a member of the Million Dollar Club?
- ☐ Does he or she have advanced designations, like Certified Real Estate Specialist?
- ☐ Does he or she know the community?
- ☐ Does he or she know a lot about mortgages—where to get them quickly, which lenders offer the best terms?
- ☐ Is he or she a skilled negotiator?
- ☐ If you're a buyer, did the agent tell you: "I will try to be fair and honest with you, but remember that I am employed by the seller and I am ethically and legally responsible for obtaining the best price for the seller and on the best terms for the seller"?
- ☐ If you're a buyer, are you sure that the agent is willing to spend plenty of time with you and not show you three houses and try to bully you into making a decision right then and there?
- ☐ If you're a seller, does he or she have a marketing plan—a detailed strategy on how to go about selling your house?
- ☐ If you're a seller, did he or she *not* tell you that you could get a significantly higher (meaning: unrealistic) price for your house than other agents suggested you could get?
- ☐ Did the agent explain the many benefits of your obtaining a professional home inspection?

GLOSSARY

Adverse possession A way that a property owner can lose ownership if someone else regularly and openly uses that property.

Agent Someone empowered to work on someone else's behalf. A real estate agent can be a salesperson or a broker.

Amperage The flow of electricity through wire.

Anti-oxidant compound A compound applied to aluminum wiring at the connections to promote a firm connection and seal it.

Anchor bolt Bolts imbedded in the foundation, to which framing (the sill plate) is fastened.

Appraisal A professional evaluation of the market value of a property.

Apron A paved area, such as a junction of a driveway with the street or with a garage entrance.

Appreciation An increase in the value of assets.

Aquastat Heat-sensing device submerged in water and used to control the operation of an appliance.

As is Without any guarantees as to the condition of a property.

Assessed value The value of a property as set by a municipal tax assessor for tax purposes.

Automatic flue damper A device in the flue of a heating unit that closes the flue when the unit is not working, to prevent heat loss up the chimney.

Baffle A device used as a heat shield or regulator, to deflect or guide the products of combustion to or away from a certain point.

Ballcock assembly The mechanism inside a toilet tank that controls the flushing of a toilet.

Berm A built-up lip of asphalt or concrete, to prevent runoff water from entering a garage or driveway.

Bi-level A "split ranch," with the lower level more out of the ground than in the ground.

Binder A preliminary agreement between a buyer and a seller.

Bracing Technique used to stiffen a building.

Broker A real estate agent who can open his or her own office; salespeople work for brokers.

Building code A community's regulations governing new construction.

Cape Cod A type of one-and-a-half–story house, common in the Northeast.

Casement window A window that opens, usually outwards, on hinges at the vertical edge.

Caveat emptor The notion that buyers purchase any articles with no guarantee as to their condition, unless any defects were not easily noticable. "Let the buyer beware."

Chimney cap Concrete "hat" around the top of the chimney brick to protect the masonry from the rain and other elements.

Cleanout An opening in the drainage system for the removal of obstructions.

Closing A meeting where ownership of property is transferred between a buyer and seller.

Colonial A traditional two-story house with an entrance hall, smaller windows upstairs than downstairs, a partially finished basement, and so forth.

Condominium A dwelling in which each unit is owned by an individual rather than by an overall landlord, and in which the unit owner has an interest in the common areas.

Conduit A metallic or nonmetallic pipe or tubing that holds electrical conductors.

Contingency clause A statement inserted into a contract that permits the cancellation of the contract unless a certain condition is met, such as the buyer's home inspector finding no significant defects in the house.

Contemporary Any modern house that doesn't easily fit into conventional house styles.

Cornice The decorative finish that projects at the top of a wall.

Crawl space A space between the soil and the lowest floor-framing part of a building.

Deed A written instrument executed and delivered to the buyer to pass title to real property.

Deposit An amount of money paid by a buyer upon signing a contractor to purchase a house.

Dip tube Extension of the water-supply line into a water-storage tank, which delivers water close to the heat source on the bottom of a water heater.

Drain valve Device used to drain water-storage tank for maintenance or replacement.

Drip loop A loop in the service conductor to minimize the chance of water penetration.

Duct A tube conveying air from a heating or cooling unit to individual rooms.

Duplex Two units sharing one roof. Also, an apartment with rooms on two floors.

Duplex receptable An electrical outlet designed to accept two lighting or appliance plugs.

Easement A right to the limited use of land owned by someone else.

Eave The part of a roof that extends beyond the house.

Encroachment An extension of a building or other installation between its owner's property line onto another owner's property.

Encumbrance A condition that limits title to property.

Escrow The placing of money with a third party to be held until transfer of title.

Fascia A flat, horizontal member of a cornice, placed in a vertical position, from which gutters are hung.

Flashing Strips of metal or other protective materials used to cover joints or angles, as on walls and roofs, for waterproofing.

Floating slab A concrete floor that isn't connected to the foundation wall.

Flue A pipe to conduct products of combustion to a chimney.

Footing A below-grade base, usually of concrete, which carries the load of a foundation, pier, or column to the ground.

Foundation The supporting construction, wholly or partly underground, of a building.

General-purpose circuit An electrical circuit that supplies a number of outlets for lighting or small appliances.

Grade On ground level.

Ground A conducting connection between an electrical circuit or equipment and the earth.

Ground fault circuit interruptor (GFCI) A fast-acting safety device, used on circuits threatened by water, to prevent serious shocks.

Gutter Channel along the eaves of a roof that carries away rainwater.

Guy A cable for steadying, guiding or holding something, like an antenna.

Handyman's special A house in poor condition.

Header A framing member across the top of an opening to distribute a load.

Home or house inspector A professional who can evaluate the structural soundness and operating systems of a residence, recommend repairs, and estimate their costs.

Improvement A change that materially adds to the value of a house, appreciably prolongs its useful life, or adapts it to new uses.

Inspection A professional evaluation of the condition of the major elements of a property.

Joist A horizontal structural member (like a wooden board) that supports a floor or ceiling, while resting on a foundation or other support.

Jamb Upright surface that lines an opening for a door.

Key A groove in the top of a footing.

Lally column A circular pipe, often filled with concrete, to support girders and beams.

Leader Pipe that carries rainwater from the gutters to the ground, to sewers, or to dry wells.

Lien A claim upon property as security for a debt.

Main girder The main support that runs between foundation walls to carry the weight of a floor.

Mechanics's lien A lien against land and buildings favoring workers who have furnished either materials or labor, but claim not to have been paid.

Meter A device to measure electrical current flow or water flow to a property.

Meter pan A piece of equipment through which the service conductor runs.

Monolithic slab A slab that's part of the footings. Usually found in houses built on stable soil in warm climates.

P trap A device that provides a liquid seal to prevent the emission of sewage gases. Shaped like the letter P.

Panel Electrical equipment with circuit breakers or fuses, terminals, and so forth, to which household wiring is connnected.

Parge coat A coating of a foundation wall to slow down passage of water.

Perc test A test to determine the soil's drainage capability, performed before the installation of a septic system. Also called a percolation test or soil percolation test.

Pier A vertical column, usually of masonry or concrete.

Pilot The flame or electronic control that ignites gas or oil burners.

Preclosing inspection A buyer walk-through inspection performed just before property changes hands.

Rafter One of a series of structural members designed to support roof loads.

Ranch A one-story house that fosters outdoors living.

Realtor A real estate broker who belongs to the National Association of Realtors.

Repair A change that merely maintains your home in an ordinary, efficient operating condition.

Restriction A limitation on the use of a property.

Ridge board The upright horizontal board at the ridge, to which the top ends of rafters are attached.

Right of way The right of one person or company to pass over or use another's land. Also, the land so used.

Roof sheathing Flat boards nailed to the rafters, to which a covering is fastened.

Sacrificial anode Metal rod inserted into a water heater. It corrodes faster than the other metals in the tank, extending the life of the tank.

Service conductor The wires that extend from the utility company's line to the house's service equipment.

Service entrance conductor The wire between the terminals of the panel and their connection with the service conductor.

Sheathing Sheets of a material applied across floors, rafters, or studs.

Siding The covering on the outside walls of a house.

Sill plate Horizontal framing on the top of a foundation wall.

Sill sealer A material that seals gaps between the foundation and the sill plate.

Slab foundation A foundation made of concrete in large sections.

Soffit The visible horizontal underside of the eave, or overhang of a house.

Sole plate The bottom horizontal member of a frame wall on which the studs sit.

Split level A house with two levels, where you step up or down as you enter.

Stud An upright framing member, typically wood.

Subflooring Material nailed to the floor joists, on top of which is the finished flooring.

Sump pump An automatic pump installed in a basement to pump out seeping groundwater.

Survey A map or a tract of land showing its size, form, boundaries, improvements, elevation, and position relative to neighboring tracts.

Swale A wide, shallow depression in the ground to channel drainage of storm water.

Thermocouple A thick copper wire that acts as a safety device on a gas burner. If the pilot light for the burner goes out, the sensor on the end of the wire cools and prevents the flow of gas to the burner.

Thermostatic control Device used to regulate the point at which the burner or energy source for a water heater is activated.

Title Proof of ownership of real property.

Toilet seal A gasket, usually wax, to seal the joint between the bottom of a toilet and the drain piping, to prevent water leakage and escape of sewer gases.

Townhouse A house sharing a wall with another house, often in a condominium-type arrangement.

TPRV (temperature/pressure relief valve) A safety device to release built-up energy in a tank at a certain temperature or pressure.

Tudor An English-style house with stucco and half-timber siding, slate roofs, angular chimneys, and gables.

Vapor barrier A material, like plastic, to prevent the passage of moisture.

Vent A pipe that provides air to and from a drainage system.

Victorian A nineteenth century house style, typically with large porches, fancy bay windows, and elaborate wooden decorations.

Voltage Pressure behind the flow of electricity.

Water table Level below which the ground is saturated with water.

Weatherhead A watertight piece of equipment where the overhead horizontal service-entrance conductor becomes vertical.

Zoning Restrictions placed on a property by local government to control area developments (to keep residences away from businesses, for example).

INDEX